CLASSIC SERIES

Greatest
Love Stories

V&S PUBLISHERS

Published by:

V&S PUBLISHERS

F-2/16, Ansari road, Daryaganj, New Delhi-110002
☎ 23240026, 23240027 • *Fax:* 011-23240028
Email: info@vspublishers.com • *Website:* www.vspublishers.com

Regional Office : Hyderabad

5-1-707/1, Brij Bhawan (Beside Central Bank of India Lane)
Bank Street, Koti, Hyderabad - 500 095
☎ 040-24737290
E-mail: vspublishershyd@gmail.com

Branch Office : Mumbai

Godown # 34 at The Model Co-Operative Housing, Society Ltd.,
"Sahakar Niwas", Ground Floor, Next to Sobo Central, Mumbai - 400 034
☎ 022-22098268
E-mail: vspublishersmum@gmail.com

Follow us on:

For any assistance sms **VSPUB** to **56161**

All books available at **www.vspublishers.com**

© **Copyright:** *V&S* PUBLISHERS
ISBN 978-93-505710-4-0
Edition 2014

Printed at : Param Offseters, Okhla, New Delhi-110020

Publisher's Note

It has been our constant endeavour at the **V&S Publishers** to publish all kinds of books ranging from Fiction, Non-fiction, Storybooks, Children Encyclopaedias, to Self-Help, Science Books, Dictionaries, Grammar Books, Self-Development, Management Books, etc.

However, this is for the first time that we are venturing into the vast, rich and fathomless ocean of English Literature and have come up with a set *of ten storybooks called the Greatest Classic Series* authored by some of the greatest and eminent writers of the world. There is a lot to learn from their writing style, selection of plot, development and building of theme and suspense of the story, emphasis and presentation of characters, dialogues, working towards the climax of the story, presenting the climax, and then finally concluding the story.

Each these books are of about 200 pages containing around ten popular stories or more of renowned authors like Oscar Wilde, Ernest William Hornung, Guy de Maupassant, O. Henry, Saki, Washington Irving, Thomas Hardy, Charles Dickens, Jules Verne, Jack London, Mark Twain, Edgar Allen Poe, H.G.Wells, Ambrose Bierce, Amelia Edwards, Edith Wharton, Wilkie Collins and many more. The series is called The Greatest Classic Series as all the names of the books begin with the word, `Greatest' like the Greatest Adventurous Stories, Greatest Detective Stories, Greatest Love Stories, Greatest Ghost Stories, and so on. Besides this, three of the ten books are exclusively on the Adventures of Sherlock Holmes, one of the best detectives the world has ever known written by none other than Sir Arthur Conan Doyle.

Besides the above mentioned characteristics, the books contain an introductory page before each story introducing the author, his brief life history, notable works and literary achievements. Each story has a set of word meanings on each page followed by an exercise meant exclusively aiming the school students to help them grasp the essence of the story easily and quickly.

These books are not only a boon for the school-going students, particularly studying in senior classes from the seventh standard till the twelfth, but are also a treasure trove for all those young and aspiring writers, voracious readers and lovers of English language and literature.

Each of these ten books focus on a theme, such as adventure, love, terror, humour, or supernatural happenings, and are so captivating and real to life that readers may find it difficult to choose from them and so it's better to pick the entire series.

Wishing you all a happy and enjoyable reading...

Contents

Edith Wharton

Born on January 24, 1862

Died on August 11, 1937

Notable works: *The Age of Innocence, The House of Mirth, Italian Villas and Their Gardens, The Glimpses of the Moon* and many short stories for children, particularly the Ghost stories

Honours: *Chevalier of the Legion of Honor in 1916, the 1921 Pulitzer Prize for Literature, etc.*

Early Life

Edith Wharton was born as Edith Newbold Jones on January 24, 1862 in New York City. Her father was George Frederic Jones and mother, Lucretia Stevens Rhinelander. She had two brothers, Frederic Rhinelander and Henry Edward. She was also related to the Rensselaer family, the most prestigious of the old patron families. Edith had a lifelong friendship with her Rhinelander niece, landscape architect Beatrix Farrand of Reef Point inBar Harbor, Maine, and often travelled with Henry James in Europe. She was well acquainted with many of her era's other literary and public figures, including Theodore Roosevelt.

In 1885, at 23 years of age, she married Edward (Teddy) Robbins Wharton, who was 12 years older than her. He shared her love of travel, although they had little in common intellectually. From the late 1880s until 1902, he suffered from acute mental depression,

Literary Works and Achievements

Edith was also a **garden designer, interior designer**, and taste-maker of her time. In 1902, she built, **The Mount**, her estate in Lenox, Massachusetts, which survives even today as an example of her design principles. There, she wrote several of her **novels**, including *The House of Mirth* in 1905. Edith wrote a number of **design books**, including her first published work, *The Decoration of Houses* of 1897, co-authored by Ogden Codman. Another is the generously illustrated *Italian Villas and Their Gardens* of 1904. In addition to novels, she wrote at least **85 short stories.**

Throughout the war, Edith worked tirelessly in charitable efforts for refugees and, in 1916 was named a *Chevalier* of the ***Legion of Honor*** in recognition of her commitment to the displaced. In 1916, Edith edited *The Book of the Homeless,* which composed of writings, art and musical scores by almost every major contemporary European artist. After World War I, she travelled to Morocco as the guest of the resident general, Gen. Hubert Lyautey and wrote a book, *In Morocco*, about her experiences.

After the war, she divided her time between Paris and Hyères, Provence, where she completed her famous book, *The Age of Innocence* in 1920 for which she won the **1921 Pulitzer Prize for literature**. This made Edith Wharton the first woman to win this award. She received an **honorary doctorate** degree from the Yale University (USA) in 1923. She spoke fluent French and many of her books were published in both French and English.

Writing Style

Many of Wharton's novels are characterised by a subtle use of dramatic irony. Having grown up in the upper-class pre-World War I society, Wharton became one of its most astute critics, in her works, such as: *The House of Mirth* and *The Age of Innocence*. In addition to writing several well-known novels, Wharton produced a wealth of short stories, particularly the ghost stories, which are extensively popular among children of all ages across the globe.

Later Years

In 1934, Wharton's autobiography – *A Backward Glance* was published. Edith Wharton died of a stroke in 1937 at the domaine *Le Pavillon Colombe*, her 18th-century house on Rue de Montmorency in Saint-Brice-sous-Forêt at the age of 78. The street is today called Edith Wharton Street. She was buried in the American Cemetery in Versailles, France.

Trivia

Edith Wharton was the second cousin of actress Verree Teasdale and was inducted into the National Women's Hall of Fame in 1996.

The House Of The Dead Hand
~ Edith Wharton

I

"Above all," the letter ended, "don't leave Siena without seeing Doctor Lombard's Leonardo. Lombard is a queer old Englishman, a *mystic* or a madman (if the two are not synonymous), and a *devout* student of the Italian Renaissance. He has lived for years in Italy, exploring its remotest corners, and has lately picked up an undoubted Leonardo, which came to light in a farmhouse near Bergamo. It is believed to be one of the missing pictures mentioned by Vasari, and is at any rate, according to the most competent authorities, a genuine and almost untouched example of the best period.

"Lombard is a queer stick, and jealous of showing his treasures; but we struck up a friendship when I was working on the Sodomas in Siena three years ago, and if you will give him the enclosed line you may get a peep at the Leonardo. Probably not more than a peep, though, for I hear he refuses to have it reproduced. I want badly to use it in my monograph on the Windsor drawings, so please see what you can do for me, and if you can't *persuade* him to let you take a photograph or make a sketch, at least jot down a detailed description of the picture and get from him all the facts you can. I hear that the French and Italian governments have offered him a large advance on his purchase, but that he refuses to sell at any price, though he certainly can't afford such luxuries; in fact, I don't see where he got enough money to buy the picture. He lives in the Via Papa Giulio."

Wyant sat at the table d'hôte of his hotel, re-reading his friend's letter over a late luncheon. He had been five days in Siena without having found time to call on Doctor Lombard; not from any indifference to the opportunity presented, but because it was his first visit to the strange red city and he was still under the spell of its more *conspicuous* wonders -- the brick palaces flinging out their wrought-iron torch-holders with a *gesture* of arrogant *suzerainty*; the great council-chamber

Suzerainty - *Position or authority*
Devout - *Pious*
Mystic – *Spiritualist*
Genuine – *Real*
Persuade – *Convince*
Conspicuous – *Obvious*
Gesture – *Sign*

emblazoned with civic allegories; the pageant of Pope Julius on the Library walls; the Sodomas smiling balefully through the dusk of mouldering chapels -- and it was only when his first hunger was appeased that he remembered that one course in the banquet was still untasted.

He put the letter in his pocket and turned to leave the room, with a nod to its only other occupant, an olive-skinned young man with lustrous eyes and a low collar, who sat on the other side of the table, perusing the Fanfulla di Domenica. This gentleman, his daily vis-a-vis, returned the nod with a Latin eloquence of gesture, and Wyant passed on to the ante-chamber, where he paused to light a cigarette. He was just restoring the case to his pocket when he heard a hurried step behind him, and the lustrous-eyed young man advanced through the glass doors of the dining room.

"Pardon me, sir," he said in measured English, and with an intonation of exquisite politeness; "you have let this letter fall."

Wyant, recognizing his friend's note of introduction to Doctor Lombard, took it with a word of thanks, and was about to turn away when he perceived that the eyes of his fellow diner remained fixed on him with a gaze of melancholic interrogation.

"Again pardon me," the young man ventured at length, "but are you by chance the friend of the illustrious Doctor Lombard?"

"No," returned Wyant, with the instinctive Anglo-Saxon distrust of foreign advances. Then, fearing to appear rude, he said with a guarded politeness, "Perhaps, by the way, you can tell me the number of his house. I see it is not given here."

The young man brightened perceptibly. "The number of the house is thirteen; but anyone can indicate it to you -- it is well known in Siena. It is called," he continued after a moment, "the House of the Dead Hand."

Wyant stared. "What a queer name!" he said.

"The name comes from an antique hand of marble which for many hundred years has been above the door."

Wyant was turning away with a gesture of thanks, when the other added, "If you would have the kindness to ring twice."

Appease – *Calm down*

Lustrous – *Shiny*

Eloquence – *Expressiveness*

Exquisite – *Beautiful*

Interrogation – *Questioning*

"To ring twice?"

"At the doctor's." The young man smiled. "It is the custom."

It was a dazzling March afternoon, with a shower of sun from the mid-blue, and a marshalling of slaty clouds behind the umber-colored hills. For nearly an hour Wyant loitered on the Lizza, watching the shadows race across the naked landscape and the thunder blacken in the west; then he decided to set out for the House of the Dead Hand. The map in his guidebook showed him that the Via Papa Giulio was one of the streets which radiate from the Piazza, and thither he bent his course, pausing at every other step to fill his eye with some fresh image of weather-beaten beauty. The clouds had rolled upward, obscuring the sunshine and hanging like a funereal baldachin above the projecting cornices of Doctor Lombard's street, and Wyant walked for some distance in the shade of the beetling palace fronts before his eye fell on a doorway surmounted by a sallow marble hand. He stood for a moment staring up at the strange emblem. The hand was a woman's -- a dead drooping hand, which hung there convulsed and helpless, as though it had been thrust forth in denunciation of some evil mystery within the house, and had sunk struggling into death.

A girl who was drawing water from the well in the court said that the English doctor lived on the first floor, and Wyant, passing through a glazed door, mounted the damp degrees of a vaulted stairway with a plaster AEsculapius mouldering in a niche on the landing. Facing the AEsculapius was another door, and as Wyant put his hand on the bell-rope he remembered his unknown friend's injunction, and rang twice.

His ring was answered by a peasant woman with a low forehead and small close-set eyes, who, after a prolonged scrutiny of himself, his card, and his letter of introduction, left him standing in a high, cold ante-chamber floored with brick. He heard her wooden pattens click down an interminable corridor, and after some delay she returned and told him to follow her.

They passed through a long saloon, bare as the ante-chamber, but loftily vaulted, and frescoed with a seventeenth-century Triumph of Scipio or Alexander -- martial figures following Wyant with the filmed melancholy gaze of shades

Custom – *Tradition*
Obscure – *Difficult to Understand*
Sallow – *Sickly*
Injunction – *Ban*
Scrutiny – *Inspection*
Interminable – *Tiresomely long*

in limbo. At the end of this apartment he was admitted to a smaller room, with the same atmosphere of mortal cold, but showing more obvious signs of occupancy. The walls were covered with tapestry which had faded to the gray-brown tints of decaying vegetation, so that the young man felt as though he were entering a sunless autumn wood. Against these hangings stood a few tall cabinets on heavy gilt feet, and at a table in the window three persons were seated: an elderly lady who was warming her hands over a brazier, a girl bent above a strip of needle-work, and an old man.

As the latter advanced towards Wyant, the young man was conscious of staring with unseemly intentness at his small round-backed figure, dressed with shabby disorder and surmounted by a wonderful head, lean, vulpine, eagle-beaked as that of some art-loving despot of the Renaissance--a head combining the venerable hair and large prominent eyes of the humanist with the greedy profile of the adventurer. Wyant, in musing on the Italian portrait-medals of the fifteenth century, had often fancied that only in that period of fierce individualism could types so paradoxical have been produced; yet the subtle craftsmen who committed them to the bronze had never drawn a face more strangely stamped with contradictory passions than that of Doctor Lombard.

"I am glad to see you," he said to Wyant, extending a hand which seemed a mere framework held together by knotted veins. "We lead a quiet life here and receive few visitors, but any friend of Professor Clyde's is welcome." Then, with a gesture which included the two women, he added dryly, "My wife and daughter often talk of Professor Clyde."

"Oh yes -- he used to make me such nice toast; they don't understand toast in Italy," said Mrs. Lombard in a high plaintive voice.

It would have been difficult, from Doctor Lombard's manner and appearance to guess his nationality; but his wife was so inconsciently and ineradicably English that even the silhouette of her cap seemed a protest against Continental laxities. She was a stout, fair woman, with pale cheeks netted with red lines. A brooch with a miniature portrait sustained a bogwood watchchain upon her bosom, and at her elbow lay a heap of knitting and an old copy of The Queen.

Shabby – *Untidy*
Musing – *Thought*
Stout – *Fat*
Replica – *Copy*
Opaque – *Solid*

The young girl, who had remained standing, was a slim replica of her mother, with an apple-cheeked face and opaque blue eyes. Her small head was prodigally laden with braids of dull fair hair, and she might have had a kind of transient prettiness but for the sullen droop of her round mouth. It was hard to say whether her expression implied ill-temper or apathy; but Wyant was struck by the contrast between the fierce vitality of the doctor's age and the inanimateness of his daughter's youth.

Seating himself in the chair which his host advanced, the young man tried to open the conversation by addressing to Mrs. Lombard some random remark on the beauties of Siena. The lady murmured a resigned assent, and Doctor Lombard interposed with a smile, "My dear sir, my wife considers Siena a most salubrious spot, and is favorably impressed by the cheapness of the marketing; but she deplores the total absence of muffins and cannel coal, and cannot resign herself to the Italian method of dusting furniture."

"But they don't, you know -- they don't dust it!" Mrs. Lombard protested, without showing any resentment of her husband's manner.

"Precisely -- they don't dust it. Since we have lived in Siena we have not once seen the cobwebs removed from the battlements of the Mangia. Can you conceive of such house-keeping? My wife has never yet dared to write it home to her aunts at Bonchurch."

Mrs. Lombard accepted in silence this remarkable state-ment of her views, and her husband, with a malicious smile at Wyant's embarrassment, planted himself suddenly before the young man. "And now," said he, "do you want to see my Leonardo?"

"*Do* I?" cried Wyant, on his feet in a flash.

The doctor chuckled. "Ah," he said, with a kind of crooning deliberation, "that's the way they all behave -- that's what they all come for." He turned to his daughter with another variation of mockery in his smile. "Don't fancy it's for your beaux yeux, my dear; or for the mature charms of Mrs. Lombard," he added, glaring suddenly at his wife, who had taken up her knitting and was softly murmuring over the number of her stitches.

Apathy – *Lack of concern*
Assent – *Consent*
Deplore – *Criticise*
Malicious – *Cruel*
Desecrate – *To damage*

Neither lady appeared to notice his pleasantries, and he continued, addressing himself to Wyant, "They all come -- they all come; but many are called and few are chosen." His voice sank to solemnity. "While I live," he said, "no unworthy eye shall desecrate that picture. But I will not do my friend Clyde the injustice to suppose that he would send an unworthy representative. He tells me he wishes a description of the picture for his book; and you shall describe it to him -- if you can."

Wyant hesitated, not knowing whether it was a propitious moment to put in his appeal for a photograph. "Well, sir," he said, "you know Clyde wants me to take away all I can of it."

Doctor Lombard eyed him sardonically. "You're welcome to take away all you can carry," he replied; adding, as he turned to his daughter, "That is, if he has your permission, Sybilla."

The girl rose without a word, and laying aside her work, took a key from a secret drawer in one of the cabinets, while the doctor continued in the same note of grim jocularity, "For you must know that the picture is not mine -- it is my daughter's."

He followed with evident amusement the surprised glance which Wyant turned on the young girl's impassive figure.

"Sybilla," he pursued, "is a votary of the arts; she has inherited her fond father's passion for the unattainable. Luckily, however, she also recently inherited a tidy legacy from her grandmother; and having seen the Leonardo, on which its discoverer had placed a price far beyond my reach, she took a step which deserves to go down to history. She invested her whole inheritance in the purchase of the picture, thus enabling me to spend my closing years in communion with one of the world's masterpieces. My dear sir, could Antigone do more?"

The object of this strange eulogy had meanwhile drawn aside one of the tapestry hangings, and fitted her key into a concealed door.

"Come," said Doctor Lombard, "let us go before the light fails us."

Wyant glanced at Mrs. Lombard, who continued to knit impassively.

"No, no," said his host, "my wife will not come with us. You might not suspect it from her conversation, but my wife

Propitious
– Favourable
Grim – Gloomy
Impassive – Unemotional
Eulogy – Tribute

has no feeling for art -- Italian art, that is; for no one is fonder of our early Victorian school."

"Frith's Railway Station, you know," said Mrs. Lombard, smiling. "I like an animated picture."

Miss Lombard, who had unlocked the door, held back the tapestry to let her father and Wyant pass out; then she followed them down a narrow stone passage with another door at its end. This door was iron-barred, and Wyant noticed that it had a complicated patent lock. The girl fitted another key into the lock, and Doctor Lombard led the way into a small room. The dark panelling of this apartment was irradiated by streams of yellow light slanting through the disbanded thunder clouds, and in the central brightness hung a picture concealed by a curtain of faded velvet.

"A little too bright, Sybilla," said Doctor Lombard. His face had grown solemn, and his mouth twitched nervously as his daughter drew a linen drapery across the upper part of the window.

"That will do -- that will do." He turned impressively to Wyant. "Do you see the pomegranate bud in this rug? Place yourself there -- keep your left foot on it, please. And now, Sybilla, draw the cord."

Miss Lombard advanced and placed her hand on a cord hidden behind the velvet curtain. "Ah," said the doctor, "one moment: I should like you, while looking at the picture, to have in mind a few lines of verse. Sybilla --"

Without the slightest change of countenance, and with a promptness which proved her to be prepared for the request, Miss Lombard began to recite, in a full round voice like her mother's, St. Bernard's invocation to the Virgin, in the thirty-third canto of the Paradise.

"Thank you, my dear," said her father, drawing a deep breath as she ended. "That unapproachable combination of vowel sounds prepares one better than anything I know for the contemplation of the picture."

As he spoke the folds of velvet slowly parted, and the Leonardo appeared in its frame of tarnished gold,

From the nature of Miss Lombard's recitation Wyant had expected a sacred subject, and his surprise was therefore great as the composition was gradually revealed by the widening division of the curtain.

Concealed – *Hidden*
Solemn – *Serious*
Countenance – *Tolerate*
Prompt – *Quick*
Contemplation – *Thought*
Sacred – *Holy*

In the background a steel-colored river wound through a pale calcareous landscape; while to the left, on a lonely peak, a crucified Christ hung livid against indigo clouds. The central figure of the foreground, however, was that of a woman seated in an antique chair of marble with bas-reliefs of dancing maenads. Her feet rested on a meadow sprinkled with minute wild flowers, and her attitude of smiling majesty recalled that of Dosso Dossi's Circe. She wore a red robe, flowing in closely fluted lines from under a fancifully embroidered cloak. Above her high forehead the crinkled golden hair flowed sideways beneath a veil; one hand drooped on the arm of her chair; the other held up an inverted human skull, into which a young Dionysus, smooth, brown and sidelong as the St. John of the Louvre, poured a stream of wine from a high-poised flagon. At the lady's feet lay the symbols of art and luxury: a flute and a roll of music, a platter heaped with grapes and roses, the torso of a Greek statuette, and a bowl overflowing with coins and jewels; behind her, on the chalky hilltop, hung the crucified Christ. A scroll in a corner of the foreground bore the legend: Lux Mundi.

Wyant, emerging from the first plunge of wonder, turned inquiringly toward his companions. Neither had moved. Miss Lombard stood with her hand on the cord, her lids lowered, her mouth drooping; the doctor, his strange Thoth-like profile turned toward his guest, was still lost in rapt contemplation of his treasure.

Wyant addressed the young girl.

"You are fortunate," he said, "to be the possessor of anything so perfect."

"It is considered very beautiful," she said coldly.

"Beautiful -- *beautiful!*" the doctor burst out. "Ah, the poor, worn out, over-worked word! There are no adjectives in the language fresh enough to describe such pristine brilliancy; all their brightness has been worn off by misuse. Think of the things that have been called beautiful, and then look at *that!*"

"It is worthy of a new vocabulary," Wyant agreed.

"Yes," Doctor Lombard continued, "my daughter is indeed fortunate. She has chosen what Catholics call the higher life -- the counsel of perfection. What other private person enjoys the same opportunity of understanding the master? Who else lives under the same roof with an untouched masterpiece of

Flagon – *Container for liquid*

Pristine – *Perfect*

Partaking – *Contribution*

Leonardo's? Think of the happiness of being always under the influence of such a creation; of living *into* it; of partaking of it in daily and hourly communion! This room is a chapel; the sight of that picture is a sacrament. What an atmosphere for a young life to unfold itself in! My daughter is singularly blessed. Sybilla, point out some of the details to Mr. Wyant; I see that he will appreciate them."

The girl turned her dense blue eyes toward Wyant; then, glancing away from him, she pointed to the canvas.

"Notice the modeling of the left hand," she began in a monotonous voice; "it recalls the hand of the Mona Lisa. The head of the naked genius will remind you of that of the St. John of the Louvre, but it is more purely pagan and is turned a little less to the right. The embroidery on the cloak is symbolic. You will see that the roots of this plant have burst through the vase. This recalls the famous definition of Hamlet's character in Wilhelm Meister. Here are the mystic rose, the flame, and the serpent, emblem of eternity. Some of the other symbols we have not yet been able to decipher."

Wyant watched her curiously; she seemed to be reciting a lesson.

"And the picture itself?" he said. "How do you explain that? Lux Mundi -- what a curious device to connect with such a subject! What can it mean?"

Miss Lombard dropped her eyes. The answer was evidently not included in her lesson.

"What, indeed?" the doctor interposed. "What does life mean? As one may define it in a hundred different ways, so one may find a hundred different meanings in this picture. Its symbolism is as many-faceted as a well-cut diamond. Who, for instance, is that divine lady? Is it she who is the true Lux Mundi -- the light reflected from jewels and young eyes, from polished marble and clear waters and statues of bronze? Or is that the Light of the World, extinguished on yonder stormy hill, and is this lady the Pride of Life, feasting blindly on the wine of iniquity, with her back turned to the light which has shone for her in vain? Something of both these meanings may be traced in the picture; but to me it symbolizes rather the central truth of existence: that all that is raised in incorruption is sown in corruption; art, beauty, love, religion; that

Emblem – *Symbol*
Interpose – *Interject*
Iniquity – *Evil,*
Wickedness

all our wine is drunk out of skulls, and poured for us by the mysterious genius of a remote and cruel past."

The doctor's face blazed. His bent figure seemed to straighten itself and become taller.

"Ah," he cried, growing more dithyrambic, "how lightly you ask what it means! How confidently you expect an answer! Yet here am I who have given my life to the study of the Renaissance; who have violated its tomb, laid open its dead body, and traced the course of every muscle, bone, and artery; who have sucked its very soul from the pages of poets and humanists; who have wept and believed with Joachim of Flora, smiled and doubted with AEneas Sylvius Piccolomini; who have patiently followed to its source the least inspiration of the masters, and groped in neolithic caverns and Babylonian ruins for the first unfolding tendrils of the arabesques of Mantegna and Crivelli; and I tell you that I stand abashed and ignorant before the mystery of this picture. It means nothing -- it means all things. It may represent the period which saw its creation; it may represent all ages past and to come. There are volumes of meaning in the tiniest emblem on the lady's cloak; the blossoms of its border are rooted in the deepest soil of myth and tradition. Don't ask what it means, young man, but bow your head in thankfulness for having seen it!"

Miss Lombard laid her hand on his arm.

"Don't excite yourself, father," she said in the detached tone of a professional nurse.

He answered with a despairing gesture. "Ah, it's easy for you to talk. You have years and years to spend with it; I am an old man, and every moment counts!"

"It's bad for you," she repeated with gentle obstinacy.

The doctor's sacred fury had in fact burnt itself out. He dropped into a seat with dull eyes and slackening lips, and his daughter drew the curtain across the picture.

Wyant turned away reluctantly. He felt that his opportunity was slipping from him, yet he dared not refer to Clyde's wish for a photograph. He now understood the meaning of the laugh with which Doctor Lombard had given him leave to carry away all the details he could remember. The picture was so dazzling, so unexpected, so crossed with elusive and contradictory suggestions, that the most alert observer, when placed suddenly before it, must lose his coordinating faculty

Abash – *Humiliate*

Obstinacy – *Stubbornness*

Enigmatic – *Mysterious*

in a sense of confused wonder. Yet how valuable to Clyde the record of such a work would be! In some ways it seemed to be the summing up of the master's thought, the key to his enigmatic philosophy.

The doctor had risen and was walking slowly toward the door. His daughter unlocked it, and Wyant followed them back in silence to the room in which they had left Mrs. Lombard. That lady was no longer there, and he could think of no excuse for lingering.

He thanked the doctor, and turned to Miss Lombard, who stood in the middle of the room as though awaiting further orders.

"It is very good of you," he said, "to allow one even a glimpse of such a treasure."

She looked at him with her odd directness. "You will come again?" she said quickly; and turning to her father she added, "You know what Professor Clyde asked. This gentleman cannot give him any account of the picture without seeing it again."

Doctor Lombard glanced at her vaguely; he was still like a person in a trance.

"Eh?" he said, rousing himself with an effort.

"I said, father, that Mr. Wyant must see the picture again if he is to tell Professor Clyde about it," Miss Lombard repeated with extraordinary precision of tone.

Wyant was silent. He had the puzzled sense that his wishes were being divined and gratified for reasons with which he was in no way connected.

"Well, well," the doctor muttered, "I don't say no -- I don't say no. I know what Clyde wants -- I don't refuse to help him." He turned to Wyant. "You may come again -- you may make notes," he added with a sudden effort. "Jot down what occurs to you. I'm willing to concede that."

Wyant again caught the girl's eye, but its emphatic message perplexed him.

"You're very good," he said tentatively, "but the fact is the picture is so mysterious -- so full of complicated detail -- that I'm afraid no notes I could make would serve Clyde's purpose as well as -- as a photograph, say. If you would allow me --"

Glimpse – *A quick look*
Concede – *Give in*
Perplex – *Confuse*

Miss Lombard's brow darkened, and her father raised his head furiously.

"A photograph? A photograph, did you say? Good God, man, not ten people have been allowed to set foot in that room! A *photograph*?"

Wyant saw his mistake, but saw also that he had gone too far to retreat.

"I know, sir, from what Clyde has told me, that you object to having any reproduction of the picture published; but he hoped you might let me take a photograph for his personal use -- not to be reproduced in his book, but simply to give him something to work by. I should take the photograph myself, and the negative would of course be yours. If you wished it, only one impression would be struck off, and that one Clyde could return to you when he had done with it."

Doctor Lombard interrupted him with a snarl. "When he had done with it? Just so: I thank thee for that word! When it had been re-photographed, drawn, traced, autotyped, passed about from hand to hand, defiled by every ignorant eye in England, vulgarized by the blundering praise of every art-scribbler in Europe! Bah! I'd as soon give you the picture itself! Why don't you ask for that?"

"Well, sir," said Wyant calmly, "if you will trust me with it, I'll engage to take it safely to England and back, and to let no eye but Clyde's see it while it is out of your keeping."

The doctor received this remarkable proposal in silence; then he burst into a laugh.

"Upon my soul!" he said with sardonic good humor.

It was Miss Lombard's turn to look perplexedly at Wyant. His last words and her father's unexpected reply had evidently carried her beyond her depth.

"Well, sir, am I to take the picture?" Wyant smilingly pursued.

"No, young man; nor a photograph of it. Nor a sketch, either; mind that, -- nothing that can be reproduced. Sybilla," he cried with sudden passion, "swear to me that the picture shall never be reproduced! No photograph, no sketch -- now or afterward. Do you hear me?"

"Yes, father," said the girl quietly.

Sardonic – *Sarcastic*
Depth – *Deepness*
Pursue – *Follow*
Malicious – *Hateful*

"The vandals," he muttered, "the desecrators of beauty; if I thought it would ever get into their hands I'd burn it first, by God!" He turned to Wyant, speaking more quietly. "I said you might come back -- I never retract what I say. But you must give me your word that no one but Clyde shall see the notes you make."

Wyant was growing warm.

"If you won't trust me with a photograph I wonder you trust me not to show my notes!" he exclaimed. The doctor looked at him with a malicious smile.

"Humph!" he said; "would they be of much use to anybody?"

Wyant saw that he was losing ground and controlled his impatience.

"To Clyde, I hope, at any rate," he answered, holding out his hand. The doctor shook it without a trace of resentment, and Wyant added, "When shall I come, sir?"

"Tomorrow -- tomorrow morning," cried Miss Lombard, speaking suddenly.

She looked fixedly at her father, and he shrugged his shoulders.

"The picture is hers," he said to Wyant.

In the ante-chamber the young man was met by the woman who had admitted him. She handed him his hat and stick, and turned to unbar the door. As the bolt slipped back he felt a touch on his arm.

"You have a letter?" she said in a low tone.

"A letter?" He stared. "What letter?"

She shrugged her shoulders, and drew back to let him pass.

II

As Wyant emerged from the house he paused once more to glance up at its scarred brick facade. The marble hand drooped tragically above the entrance. In the waning light it seemed to have relaxed into the passiveness of despair, and Wyant stood musing on its hidden meaning. But the Dead Hand was not the only mysterious thing about Doctor Lombard's house. What were the relations between Miss Lombard and her father? Above all, between Miss Lombard and her picture? She did

Resentment – *Anger*
Despair – *Misery*
Turbulent
– *Agitation*
Ecstasy – *Immense joy/delight*

not look like a person capable of a disinterested passion for the arts; and there had been moments when it struck Wyant that she hated the picture.

The sky at the end of the street was flooded with turbulent yellow light, and the young man turned his steps toward the church of San Domenico, in the hope of catching the lingering brightness on Sodoma's St. Catherine.

The great bare aisles were almost dark when he entered, and he had to grope his way to the chapel steps. Under the momentary evocation of the sunset, the saint's figure emerged pale and swooning from the dusk, and the warm light gave a sensual tinge to her ecstasy. The flesh seemed to glow and heave, the eyelids to tremble; Wyant stood fascinated by the accidental collaboration of light and color.

Suddenly he noticed that something white had fluttered to the ground at his feet. He stooped and picked up a small thin sheet of note-paper, folded and sealed like an old-fashioned letter, and bearing the superscription:

To the Count Ottaviano Celsi.

Wyant stared at this mysterious document. Where had it come from? He was distinctly conscious of having seen it fall through the air, close to his feet. He glanced up at the dark ceiling of the chapel; then he turned and looked about the church. There was only one figure in it, that of a man who knelt near the high altar.

Suddenly Wyant recalled the question of Doctor Lombard's maidservant. Was this the letter she had asked for? Had he been unconsciously carrying it about with him all the afternoon? Who was Count Ottaviano Celsi, and how came Wyant to have been chosen to act as that nobleman's ambulant letter box?

Wyant laid his hat and stick on the chapel steps and began to explore his pockets, in the irrational hope of finding there some clue to the mystery; but they held nothing which he had not himself put there, and he was reduced to wondering how the letter, supposing some unknown hand to have bestowed it on him, had happened to fall out while he stood motionless before the picture.

At this point he was disturbed by a step on the floor of the aisle, and turning, he saw his lustrous-eyed neighbor of the table d'hôte.

Conscious – *Aware*
Bestow – *Give*
Lustrous – *Shiny*
Felicitous – *Lucky*

The young man bowed and waved an apologetic hand.

"I do not intrude?" he inquired suavely.

Without waiting for a reply, he mounted the steps of the chapel, glancing about him with the affable air of an afternoon caller.

"I see," he remarked with a smile, "that you know the hour at which our saint should be visited."

Wyant agreed that the hour was indeed felicitous.

The stranger stood beamingly before the picture.

"What grace! What poetry!" he murmured, apostrophizing the St. Catherine, but letting his glance slip rapidly about the chapel as he spoke.

Wyant, detecting the manoeuvre, murmured a brief assent.

"But it is cold here -- mortally cold; you do not find it so?" The intruder put on his hat. "It is permitted at this hour -- when the church is empty. And you, my dear sir -- do you not feel the dampness? You are an artist, are you not? And to artists it is permitted to cover the head when they are engaged in the study of the paintings."

He darted suddenly toward the steps and bent over Wyant's hat.

"Permit me -- cover yourself!" he said a moment later, holding out the hat with an ingratiating gesture. A light flashed on Wyant.

"Perhaps," he said, looking straight at the young man, "you will tell me your name. My own is Wyant."

The stranger, surprised, but not disconcerted, drew forth a coroneted card, which he offered with a low bow. On the card was engraved:

Il Conte Ottaviano Celsi

"I am much obliged to you," said Wyant; "and I may as well tell you that the letter which you apparently expected to find in the lining of my hat is not there, but in my pocket."

He drew it out and handed it to its owner, who had grown very pale.

"And now," Wyant continued, "you will perhaps be good enough to tell me what all this means."

There was no mistaking the effect produced on Count Ottaviano by this request. His lips moved, but he achieved only an ineffectual smile.

Disconcert
– *Disturb*
Engraved
– *Imprinted*
Ineffectual –
Incompetent

"I suppose you know," Wyant went on, his anger rising at the sight of the other's discomfiture, "that you have taken an unwarrantable liberty. I don't yet understand what part I have been made to play, but it's evident that you have made use of me to serve some purpose of your own, and I propose to know the reason why."

Count Ottaviano advanced with an imploring gesture.

"Sir," he pleaded, "you permit me to speak?"

"I expect you to," cried Wyant. "But not here," he added, hearing the clank of the verger's keys. "It is growing dark, and we shall be turned out in a few minutes."

He walked across the church, and Count Ottaviano followed him out into the deserted square.

"Now," said Wyant, pausing on the steps.

The Count, who had regained some measure of self-possession, began to speak in a high key, with an accompaniment of conciliatory gesture.

"My dear sir -- my dear Mr. Wyant -- you find me in an abominable position -- that, as a man of honor, I immediately confess. I have taken advantage of you -- yes! I have counted on your amiability, your chivalry -- too far, perhaps? I confess it! But what could I do? It was to oblige a lady" -- he laid a hand on his heart --"a lady whom I would die to serve!" He went on with increasing volubility, his deliberate English swept away by a torrent of Italian, through which Wyant, with some difficulty, struggled to a comprehension of the case.

Count Ottaviano, according to his own statement, had come to Siena some months previously, on business connected with his mother's property; the paternal estate being near Orvieto, of which ancient city his father was syndic. Soon after his arrival in Siena the young Count had met the incomparable daughter of Doctor Lombard, and falling deeply in love with her, had prevailed on his parents to ask her hand in marriage. Doctor Lombard had not opposed his suit, but when the question of settlements arose it became known that Miss Lombard, who was possessed of a small property in her own right, had a short time before invested the whole amount in the purchase of the Bergamo Leonardo. Thereupon Count Ottaviano's parents had politely suggested that she should sell the picture and thus recover her independence;

Abominable – *Offensive*
Amiability – *Friendliness*
Chivalry – *Politeness*
Oppose – *Be against*

and this proposal being met by a curt refusal from Doctor Lombard, they had withdrawn their consent to their son's marriage. The young lady's attitude had hitherto been one of passive submission; she was horribly afraid of her father, and would never venture openly to oppose him; but she had made known to Ottaviano her intention of not giving him up, of waiting patiently till events should take a more favorable turn. She seemed hardly aware, the Count said with a sigh, that the means of escape lay in her own hands; that she was of age, and had a right to sell the picture, and to marry without asking her father's consent. Meanwhile her suitor spared no pains to keep himself before her, to remind her that he, too, was waiting and would never give her up.

Doctor Lombard, who suspected the young man of trying to persuade Sybilla to sell the picture, had forbidden the lovers to meet or to correspond; they were thus driven to clandestine communication, and had several times, the Count ingenuously avowed, made use of the doctor's visitors as a means of exchanging letters.

"And you told the visitors to ring twice?" Wyant interposed.

The young man extended his hands in a deprecating gesture. Could Mr. Wyant blame him? He was young, he was ardent, he was enamored! The young lady had done him the supreme honor of avowing her attachment, of pledging her unalterable fidelity; should he suffer his devotion to be outdone? But his purpose in writing to her, he admitted, was not merely to reiterate his fidelity; he was trying by every means in his power to induce her to sell the picture. He had organized a plan of action; every detail was complete; if she would but have the courage to carry out his instructions he would answer for the result. His idea was that she should secretly retire to a convent of which his aunt was the Mother Superior, and from that stronghold should transact the sale of the Leonardo. He had a purchaser ready, who was willing to pay a large sum; a sum, Count Ottaviano whispered, considerably in excess of the young lady's original inheritance; once the picture sold, it could, if necessary, be removed by force from Doctor Lombard's house, and his daughter, being safely in the convent, would be spared the painful scenes incidental to the removal. Finally, if Doctor Lombard were vindictive enough to refuse his consent to her marriage, she had only to make

Gesture – *Sign*
Ardent – *Passionate*
Induce – *Persuade*
Vindictive – *Cruel*
Absurd – *Ridiculous*

Greatest   Love   Stories

a sommation respectueuse, and at the end of the prescribed delay no power on earth could prevent her becoming the wife of Count Ottaviano.

Wyant's anger had fallen at the recital of this simple romance. It was absurd to be angry with a young man who confided his secrets to the first stranger he met in the streets, and placed his hand on his heart whenever he mentioned the name of his betrothed. The easiest way out of the business was to take it as a joke. Wyant had played the wall to this new Pyramus and Thisbe, and was philosophic enough to laugh at the part he had unwittingly performed.

He held out his hand with a smile to Count Ottaviano.

"I won't deprive you any longer," he said, "of the pleasure of reading your letter."

"Oh, sir, a thousand thanks! And when you return to the casa Lombard, you will take a message from me -- the letter she expected this afternoon?"

"The letter she expected?" Wyant paused. "No, thank you. I thought you understood that where I come from we don't do that kind of thing -- knowingly."

"But, sir, to serve a young lady!"

"I'm sorry for the young lady, if what you tell me is true" -- the Count's expressive hands resented the doubt -- "but remember that if I am under obligations to anyone in this matter, it is to her father, who has admitted me to his house and has allowed me to see his picture."

"*His* picture? Hers!"

"Well, the house is his, at all events."

"Unhappily -- since to her it is a dungeon!"

"Why doesn't she leave it, then?" exclaimed Wyant impatiently.

The Count clasped his hands. "Ah, how you say that -- with what force, with what virility! If you would but say it to *her* in that tone -- you, her countryman! She has no one to advise her; the mother is an idiot; the father is terrible; she is in his power; it is my belief that he would kill her if she resisted him. Mr. Wyant, I tremble for her life while she remains in that house!"

"Oh, come," said Wyant lightly, "they seem to understand each other well enough. But in any case, you must

Resent – *Dislike*
Interfere – *Get in the way*
Amiable – *Friendly*
Gaunt – *Thin*
Evident – *Obvious*

see that I can't interfere -- at least you would if you were an Englishman," he added with an escape of contempt.

III

Wyant's affiliations in Siena being restricted to an acquaintance with his land-lady, he was forced to apply to her for the verification of Count Ottaviano's story.

The young nobleman had, it appeared, given a perfectly correct account of his situation. His father, Count Celsi-Mongirone, was a man of distinguished family and some wealth. He was syndic of Orvieto, and lived either in that town or on his neighboring estate of Mongirone. His wife owned a large property near Siena, and Count Ottaviano, who was the second son, came there from time to time to look into its management. The eldest son was in the army, the youngest in the Church; and an aunt of Count Ottaviano's was Mother Superior of the Visitandine convent in Siena. At one time it had been said that Count Ottaviano, who was a most amiable and accomplished young man, was to marry the daughter of the strange Englishman, Doctor Lombard, but difficulties having arisen as to the adjustment of the young lady's dower, Count Celsi-Mongirone had very properly broken off the match. It was sad for the young man, however, who was said to be deeply in love, and to find frequent excuses for coming to Siena to inspect his mother's estate.

Viewed in the light of Count Ottaviano's personality the story had a tinge of opera bouffe; but the next morning, as Wyant mounted the stairs of the House of the Dead Hand, the situation insensibly assumed another aspect. It was impossible to take Doctor Lombard lightly; and there was a suggestion of fatality in the appearance of his gaunt dwelling. Who could tell amid what tragic records of domestic tyranny and fluttering broken purposes the little drama of Miss Lombard's fate was being played out? Might not the accumulated influences of such a house modify the lives within it in a manner unguessed by the inmates of a suburban villa with sanitary plumbing and a telephone?

One person, at least, remained unperturbed by such fanciful problems; and that was Mrs. Lombard, who, at Wyant's

Interfere – *Intrude*
Clever – *Ascended*
Contempt –
Scorn
Inmates– *Residents*
Tyranny – *Despotism*

entrance, raised a placidly wrinkled brow from her knitting. The morning was mild, and her chair had been wheeled into a bar of sunshine near the window, so that she made a cheerful spot of prose in the poetic gloom of her surroundings.

"What a nice morning!" she said; "it must be delightful weather at Bonchurch."

Her dull blue glance wandered across the narrow street with its threatening house fronts, and fluttered back baffled, like a bird with clipped wings. It was evident, poor lady, that she had never seen beyond the opposite houses.

Wyant was not sorry to find her alone. Seeing that she was surprised at his reappearance he said at once, "I have come back to study Miss Lombard's picture."

"Oh, the picture --" Mrs. Lombard's face expressed a gentle disappointment, which might have been boredom in a person of acuter sensibilities. "It's an original Leonardo, you know," she said mechanically.

"And Miss Lombard is very proud of it, I suppose? She seems to have inherited her father's love for art."

Mrs. Lombard counted her stitches, and he went on: "It's unusual in so young a girl. Such tastes generally develop later."

Mrs. Lombard looked up eagerly. "That's what I say! I was quite different at her age, you know. I liked dancing, and doing a pretty bit of fancy-work. Not that I couldn't sketch, too; I had a master down from London. My aunts have some of my crayons hung up in their drawing room now -- I did a view of Kenilworth which was thought pleasing. But I liked a picnic, too, or a pretty walk through the woods with young people of my own age. I say it's more natural, Mr. Wyant; one may have a feeling for art, and do crayons that are worth framing, and yet not give up everything else. I was taught that there were other things."

Wyant, half-ashamed of provoking these innocent confidences, could not resist another question. "And Miss Lombard cares for nothing else?"

Her mother looked troubled.

"Sybilla is so clever -- she says I don't understand. You know how self-confident young people are! My husband never said that of me, now -- he knows I had an excellent

Eager – *Keen*
Clever – *Intelligent*
Triumphant – *Successful*
Superior – *Better*

education. My aunts were very particular; I was brought up to have opinions, and my husband has always respected them. He says himself that he wouldn't for the world miss hearing my opinion on any subject; you may have noticed that he often refers to my tastes. He has always respected my preference for living in England; he likes to hear me give my reasons for it. He is so much interested in my ideas that he often says he knows just what I am going to say before I speak. But Sybilla does not care for what I think --"

At this point Doctor Lombard entered. He glanced sharply at Wyant. "The servant is a fool; she didn't tell me you were here." His eye turned to his wife. "Well, my dear, what have you been telling Mr. Wyant? About the aunts at Bonchurch, I'll be bound!"

Mrs. Lombard looked triumphantly at Wyant, and her husband rubbed his hooked fingers, with a smile.

"Mrs. Lombard's aunts are very superior women. They subscribe to the circulating library, and borrow Good Words and the Monthly Packet from the curate's wife across the way. They have the rector to tea twice a year, and keep a page boy, and are visited by two baronets' wives. They devoted themselves to the education of their orphan niece, and I think I may say without boasting that Mrs. Lombard's conversation shows marked traces of the advantages she enjoyed."

Mrs. Lombard colored with pleasure.

"I was telling Mr. Wyant that my aunts were very particular."

"Quite so, my dear; and did you mention that they never sleep in anything but linen, and that Miss Sophia puts away the furs and blankets every spring with her own hands? Both those facts are interesting to the student of human nature." Doctor Lombard glanced at his watch. "But we are missing an incomparable moment; the light is perfect at this hour."

Wyant rose, and the doctor led him through the tapestried door and down the passageway.

The light was, in fact, perfect, and the picture shone with an inner radiancy, as though a lamp burned behind the soft screen of the lady's flesh. Every detail of the foreground detached itself with jewel-like precision. Wyant

Radiance
– *Happiness*
Precision – *Accuracy*
Devout – *Dedicated*
Contemplation –
Consideration

noticed a dozen accessories which had escaped him on the previous day.

He drew out his notebook, and the doctor, who had dropped his sardonic grin for a look of devout contemplation, pushed a chair forward, and seated himself on a carved settle against the wall.

"Now, then," he said, "tell Clyde what you can; but the letter killeth."

He sank down, his hands hanging on the arm of the settle like the claws of a dead bird, his eyes fixed on Wyant's notebook with the obvious intention of detecting any attempt at a surreptitious sketch.

Wyant, nettled at this surveillance, and disturbed by the speculations which Doctor Lombard's strange household excited, sat motionless for a few minutes, staring first at the picture and then at the blank pages of the notebook. The thought that Doctor Lombard was enjoying his discomfiture at length roused him, and he began to write.

He was interrupted by a knock on the iron door. Doctor Lombard rose to unlock it, and his daughter entered.

She bowed hurriedly to Wyant, without looking at him.

"Father, had you forgotten that the man from Monte Amiato was to come back this morning with an answer about the bas-relief? He is here now; he says he can't wait."

"The devil!" cried her father impatiently. "Didn't you tell him --"

"Yes; but he says he can't come back. If you want to see him you must come now."

"Then you think there's a chance?"

She nodded.

He turned and looked at Wyant, who was writing assiduously.

"You will stay here, Sybilla; I shall be back in a moment."

He hurried out, locking the door behind him.

Wyant had looked up, wondering if Miss Lombard would show any surprise at being locked in with him; but it was his turn to be surprised, for hardly had they heard the key withdrawn when she moved close to him, her small face pale and tumultuous.

Assiduous – *Attentive*
Tumultuous – *Confused*
Conspiracy – *Plan, Plot*

"I arranged it -- I must speak to you," she gasped. "He'll be back in five minutes."

Her courage seemed to fail, and she looked at him helplessly.

Wyant had a sense of stepping among explosives. He glanced about him at the dusky vaulted room, at the haunting smile of the strange picture overhead, and at the pink-and-white girl whispering of conspiracies in a voice meant to exchange platitudes with a curate.

"How can I help you?" he said with a rush of compassion.

"Oh, if you would! I never have a chance to speak to anyone; it's so difficult -- he watches me -- he'll be back immediately."

"Try to tell me what I can do."

"I don't dare; I feel as if he were behind me." She turned away, fixing her eyes on the picture. A sound startled her. "There he comes, and I haven't spoken! It was my only chance; but it bewilders me so to be hurried."

"I don't hear anyone," said Wyant, listening. "Try to tell me."

"How can I make you understand? It would take so long to explain." She drew a deep breath, and then with a plunge --"Will you come here again this afternoon -- at about five?" she whispered.

"Come here again?"

"Yes -- you can ask to see the picture, -- make some excuse. He will come with you, of course; I will open the door for you -- and -- and lock you both in" -- she gasped.

"Lock us in?"

"You see? You understand? It's the only way for me to leave the house -- if I am ever to do it" -- She drew another difficult breath. "The key will be returned -- by a safe person -- in half an hour, -- perhaps sooner --"

She trembled so much that she was obliged to lean against the settle for support.

Wyant looked at her steadily; he was very sorry for her.

"I can't, Miss Lombard," he said at length.

"You can't?"

"I'm sorry; I must seem cruel; but consider --"

Plunge – *Fall*
Futility – *Uselessness*
Facade – *Pretence*

He was stopped by the futility of the word, as well ask a hunted rabbit to pause in its dash for a hole!

Wyant took her hand; it was cold and nerveless.

"I will serve you in any way I can; but you must see that this way is impossible. Can't I talk to you again? Perhaps --"

"Oh," she cried, starting up, "there he comes!"

Doctor Lombard's step sounded in the passage.

Wyant held her fast. "Tell me one thing: he won't let you sell the picture?"

"No -- hush!"

"Make no pledges for the future, then; promise me that."

"The future?"

"In case he should die, your father is an old man. You haven't promised?"

She shook her head.

"Don't then; remember that."

She gave no answer, and the key turned in the lock.

As he passed out of the house, its scowling cornice and facade of ravaged brick looked down on him with the startlingness of a strange face, seen momentarily in a crowd, and impressing itself on the brain as part of an inevitable future. Above the doorway, the marble hand reached out like the cry of an imprisoned anguish.

Wyant turned away impatiently.

"Rubbish!" he said to himself. "*She* isn't walled in; she can get out if she wants to."

IV

Wyant had any number of plans for coming to Miss Lombard's aid. He was elaborating the twentieth when, on the same afternoon, he stepped into the express train for Florence. By the time the train reached Certaldo he was convinced that, in thus hastening his departure, he had followed the only reasonable course; at Empoli, he began to reflect that the priest and the Levite had probably justified themselves in much the same manner.

A month later, after his return to England, he was unexpectedly relieved from these alternatives of extenuation and approval. A paragraph in the morning paper announced the

Dilettante
– Amateur
Perspicacity –
Sharpness, Keenness
Compunction
– Regret, Remorse
Ardor *– Passion,*
Fervour

sudden death of Doctor Lombard, the distinguished English dilettante who had long resided in Siena. Wyant's justification was complete. Our blindest impulses become evidence of perspicacity when they fall in with the course of events.

Wyant could now comfortably speculate on the particular complications from which his foresight had probably saved him. The climax was unexpectedly dramatic. Miss Lombard, on the brink of a step which, whatever its issue, would have burdened her with retrospective compunction, had been set free before her suitor's ardor could have had time to cool, and was now doubtless planning a life of domestic felicity on the proceeds of the Leonardo. One thing, however, struck Wyant as odd -- he saw no mention of the sale of the picture. He had scanned the papers for an immediate announcement of its transfer to one of the great museums; but presently concluding that Miss Lombard, out of filial piety, had wished to avoid an appearance of unseemly haste in the disposal of her treasure, he dismissed the matter from his mind. Other affairs happened to engage him; the months slipped by, and gradually the lady and the picture dwelt less vividly in his mind.

It was not till five or six years later, when chance took him again to Siena, that the recollection started from some inner fold of memory. He found himself, as it happened, at the head of Doctor Lombard's street, and glancing down that grim thoroughfare, caught an oblique glimpse of the doctor's house front, with the Dead Hand projecting above its threshold. The sight revived his interest, and that evening, over an admirable frittata, he questioned his landlady about Miss Lombard's marriage.

"The daughter of the English doctor? But she has never married, signore."

"Never married? What, then, became of Count Ottaviano?"

"For a long time he waited; but last year he married a noble lady of the Maremma."

"But what happened -- why was the marriage broken?"

The landlady enacted a pantomime of baffled interrogation.

"And Miss Lombard still lives in her father's house?"

"Yes, signore; she is still there."

"And the Leonardo --"

"The Leonardo, also, is still there."

Oblique – *Slanted*
Baffled – *Puzzled*
Interrogation –
Questioning
Resolve – *Decide*
Imminent – *Coming up, conpending*

The next day, as Wyant entered the House of the Dead Hand, he remembered Count Ottaviano's injunction to ring twice, and smiled mournfully to think that so much subtlety had been vain. But what could have prevented the marriage? If Doctor Lombard's death had been long delayed, time might have acted as a dissolvent, or the young lady's resolve have failed; but it seemed impossible that the white heat of ardor in which Wyant had left the lovers should have cooled in a few short weeks.

As he ascended the vaulted stairway the atmosphere of the place seemed a reply to his conjectures. The same numbing air fell on him, like an emanation from some persistent will-power, a something fierce and imminent which might reduce to impotence every impulse within its range. Wyant could almost fancy a hand on his shoulder, guiding him upward with the ironical intent of confronting him with the evidence of its work.

A strange servant opened the door, and he was presently introduced to the tapestried room, where, from their usual seats in the window, Mrs. Lombard and her daughter advanced to welcome him with faint ejaculations of surprise.

Both had grown oddly old, but in a dry, smooth way, as fruits might shrivel on a shelf instead of ripening on the tree. Mrs. Lombard was still knitting, and pausing now and then to warm her swollen hands above the brazier; and Miss Lombard, in rising, had laid aside a strip of needle-work which might have been the same on which Wyant had first seen her engaged.

Their visitor inquired discreetly how they had fared in the interval, and learned that they had thought of returning to England, but had somehow never done so.

"I am sorry not to see my aunts again," Mrs. Lombard said resignedly; "but Sybilla thinks it best that we should not go this year."

"Next year, perhaps," murmured Miss Lombard, in a voice which seemed to suggest that they had a great waste of time to fill.

She had returned to her seat, and sat bending over her work. Her hair enveloped her head in the same thick braids, but the rose color of her cheeks had turned to blotches of dull red, like some pigment which has darkened in drying.

Startle – *Surprise*
Assure – *Promise*
Ensue – *Result,*
Emerge, Emanate
Assent – *Agree*

"And Professor Clyde -- is he well?" Mrs. Lombard asked affably; continuing, as her daughter raised a startled eye, "Surely, Sybilla, Mr. Wyant was the gentleman who was sent by Professor Clyde to see the Leonardo?"

Miss Lombard was silent, but Wyant hastened to assure the elder lady of his friend's well-being.

"Ah -- perhaps, then, he will come back some day to Siena," she said, sighing. Wyant declared that it was more than likely; and there ensued a pause, which he presently broke by saying to Miss Lombard, "And you still have the picture?"

She raised her eyes and looked at him. "Should you like to see it?" she asked.

On his assenting, she rose, and extracting the same key from the same secret drawer, unlocked the door beneath the tapestry. They walked down the passage in silence, and she stood aside with a grave gesture, making Wyant pass before her into the room. Then she crossed over and drew the curtain back from the picture.

The light of the early afternoon poured full on it. Its surface appeared to ripple and heave with a fluid splendor. The colors had lost none of their warmth, the outlines none of their pure precision; it seemed to Wyant like some magical flower which had burst suddenly from the mould of darkness and oblivion.

He turned to Miss Lombard with a movement of comprehension.

"Ah, I understand -- you couldn't part with it, after all!" he cried.

"No -- I couldn't part with it," she answered.

"It's too beautiful, -- too beautiful," -- he assented.

"Too beautiful?" She turned on him with a curious stare. "I have never thought it beautiful, you know."

He gave back the stare. "You have never --"

She shook her head. "It's not that. I hate it; I've always hated it. But he wouldn't let me -- he will never let me now."

Wyant was startled by her use of the present tense. Her look surprised him, too. There was a strange fixity of resentment in her innocuous eye. Was it possible that she was labouring under some delusion? Or did the pronoun not refer to her father?

"You mean that Doctor Lombard did not wish you to part with the picture?"

Delusion - *False belief or opinion*
Comprehension – *Understanding, Perception*
Stare – *Look intently*
Resentment – *Hatred*
Innocuous – *Harmless*

"No -- he prevented me; he will always prevent me."

There was another pause. "You promised him, then, before his death --"

"No; I promised nothing. He died too suddenly to make me." Her voice sank to a whisper. "I was free -- perfectly free -- or I thought I was till I tried."

"Till you tried?"

"To disobey him -- to sell the picture. Then I found it was impossible. I tried again and again; but he was always in the room with me."

She glanced over her shoulder as though she had heard a step; and to Wyant, too, for a moment, the room seemed full of a third presence.

"And you can't" -- he faltered, unconsciously dropping his voice to the pitch of hers.

She shook her head, gazing at him mystically. "I can't lock him out; I can never lock him out now. I told you I should never have another chance."

Wyant felt the chill of her words like a cold breath in his hair.

"Oh" -- he groaned; but she cut him off with a grave gesture.

"It is too late," she said; "but you ought to have helped me that day."

Food For Thought

What is the symbolism of a sculpture of a woman's dead hand hanging over the door of the house in the story? What does it signify? Read about the author, Edith Wharton and describe how her life is related to the essence of this story?

An Understanding

Q. 1. What was the travelling visitor looking for in Italy? What does his friend want him to look at?

Ans. _____

_____

_____

_____

_____

Q. 2. Why was the pretentious Doctor Lombard so possessive about the painting? What was the painting all about and who looked after it after Doctor Lombard's death?

Ans. _____

_____

_____

_____

_____

Q. 3. Why did Doctor Lombard's daughter hate the painting? What kind of a story is this?

Ans. _____

_____

_____

_____

_____

Q. 4. Why did the author, Edith Wharton chose Italy as the base of her story? Why was the house called 'The House of the Dead Hand'?

Ans. _____

_____

_____

_____

_____

The Fulness Of Life

~ Edith Wharton

I

FOr hours she had lain in a kind of gentle *torpor*, not unlike that sweet lassitude which masters one in the hush of a midsummer noon, when the heat seems to have silenced the very birds and insects, and, lying sunk in the tasselled meadow grasses, one looks up through a level roofing of maple leaves at the vast shadowless, and unsuggestive blue. Now and then, at ever-lengthening intervals, a flash of pain darted through her, like the ripple of sheet-lightning across such a midsummer sky; but it was too transitory to shake her stupor, that calm, delicious, bottomless stupor into which she felt herself sinking more and more deeply, without a disturbing impulse of resistance, an effort of reattachment to the vanishing edges of consciousness.

The resistance, the effort, had known their hour of violence; but now they were at an end. Through her mind, long harried by grotesque visions, fragmentary images of the life that she was leaving, tormenting lines of verse, obstinate presentiments of pictures once beheld, indistinct impressions of rivers, towers, and cupolas, gathered in the length of journeys half forgotten through her mind there now only moved a few primal sensations of colorless well-being; a vague satisfaction in the thought that she had swallowed her noxious last draught of medicine . . . and that she should never again hear the creaking of her husband's boots -- those horrible boots -- and that no one would come to bother her about the next day's dinner . . . or the butcher's book. . . .

At last even these dim sensations spent themselves in the thickening obscurity which enveloped her; a dusk now filled with pale geometric roses, circling softly, interminably before her, now darkened to a uniform blue-blackness, the hue of a summer night without stars. And into this darkness she felt herself sinking, sinking, with the gentle sense of security of one upheld from beneath. Like a tepid tide it rose around her, gliding ever higher and higher, folding in its velvety embrace

Staupor - *Absence or suppression of passion*
Torpor - *Sluggish in activity*
Interval – *Gap*
Grotesque – *Ugly*
Torment – *Torture*
Vague – *Unclear*
Obscurity – *Darkness*
Tepid – *Indifferent*

her relaxed and tired body, now submerging her breast and shoulders, now creeping gradually, with soft inexorableness, over her throat to her chin, to her ears, to her mouth. . . . Ah, now it was rising too high; the impulse to struggle was renewed; . . . her mouth was full; . . . she was choking. . . . Help!

"It is all over," said the nurse, drawing down the eyelids with official composure.

The clock struck three. They remembered it afterward. Someone opened the window and let in a blast of that strange, neutral air which walks the earth between darkness and dawn; someone else led the husband into another room. He walked vaguely, like a blind man, on his creaking boots.

II

She stood, as it seemed, on a threshold, yet no tangible gateway was in front of her. Only a wide vista of light, mild yet penetrating as the gathered glimmer of innumerable stars, expanded gradually before her eyes, in blissful contrast to the cavernous darkness from which she had of late emerged.

She stepped forward, not frightened, but hesitating, and as her eyes began to grow more familiar with the melting depths of light about her, she distinguished the outlines of a landscape, at first swimming in the opaline uncertainty of Shelley's vaporous creations, then gradually resolved into distincter shape -- the vast unrolling of a sunlit plain, aerial forms of mountains, and presently the silver crescent of a river in the valley, and a blue stencilling of trees along its curve -- something suggestive in its ineffable hue of an azure background of Leonardo's, strange, enchanting, mysterious, leading on the eye and the imagination into regions of fabulous delight. As she gazed, her heart beat with a soft and rapturous surprise; so exquisite a promise she read in the summons of that hyaline distance.

"And so death is not the end after all," in sheer gladness she heard herself exclaiming aloud. "I always knew that it couldn't be. I believed in Darwin, of course. I do still; but then Darwin himself said that he wasn't sure about the soul -- at least, I think he did -- and Wallace was a spiritualist; and then there was St. George Mivart --"

Inexorableness – *Unavoidability*
Composure – *Calm*
Contrast – *Difference*
Exquisite – *Beautiful*
Ethereal – *Ghostly*

Her gaze lost itself in the ethereal remoteness of the mountains.

"How beautiful! How satisfying!" she murmured. "Perhaps now I shall really know what it is to live."

As she spoke she felt a sudden thickening of her heart-beats, and looking up she was aware that before her stood the Spirit of Life.

"Have you never really known what it is to live?" the Spirit of Life asked her.

"I have never known," she replied, "that fulness of life which we all feel ourselves capable of knowing; though my life has not been without scattered hints of it, like the scent of earth which comes to one sometimes far out at sea."

"And what do you call the fulness of life?" the Spirit asked again.

"Oh, I can't tell you, if you don't know," she said, almost reproachfully. "Many words are supposed to define it -- love and sympathy are those in commonest use, but I am not even sure that they are the right ones, and so few people really know what they mean."

"You were married," said the Spirit, "yet you did not find the fulness of life in your marriage?"

"Oh, dear, no," she replied, with an indulgent scorn, "my marriage was a very incomplete affair."

"And yet you were fond of your husband?"

"You have hit upon the exact word; I was fond of him, yes, just as I was fond of my grandmother, and the house that I was born in, and my old nurse. Oh, I was fond of him, and we were counted a very happy couple. But I have sometimes thought that a woman's nature is like a great house full of rooms; there is the hall, through which everyone passes in going in and out; the drawing room, where one receives formal visits; the sitting room, where the members of the family come and go as they list; but beyond that, far beyond, are other rooms, the handles of whose doors perhaps are never turned; no one knows the way to them, no one knows whither they lead; and in the innermost room, the holy of holies, the soul sits alone and waits for a footstep that never comes."

Reproach – *Blame*
Scorn – *Disrespect*
Impatient
– *Intolerant*

"And your husband," asked the Spirit, after a pause, "never got beyond the family sitting room?"

"Never," she returned, impatiently; "and the worst of it was that he was quite content to remain there. He thought it perfectly beautiful, and sometimes, when he was admiring its commonplace furniture, insignificant as the chairs and tables of a hotel parlor, I felt like crying out to him, 'Fool, will you never guess that close at hand are rooms full of treasures and wonders, such as the eye of man hath not seen, rooms that no step has crossed, but that might be yours to live in, could you but find the handle of the door?'"

"Then," the Spirit continued, "those moments of which you lately spoke, which seemed to come to you like scattered hints of the fulness of life, were not shared with your husband?"

"Oh, no -- never. He was different. His boots creaked, and he always slammed the door when he went out, and he never read anything but railway novels and the sporting advertisements in the papers -- and -- and, in short, we never understood each other in the least."

"To what influence, then, did you owe those exquisite sensations?"

"I can hardly tell. Sometimes to the perfume of a flower; sometimes to a verse of Dante or of Shakespeare; sometimes to a picture or a sunset, or to one of those calm days at sea, when one seems to be lying in the hollow of a blue pearl; sometimes, but rarely, to a word spoken by someone who chanced to give utterance, at the right moment, to what I felt but could not express." "Someone whom you loved?" asked the Spirit.

"I never loved anyone, in that way," she said, rather sadly, "nor was I thinking of any one person when I spoke, but of two or three who, by touching for an instant upon a certain chord of my being, had called forth a single note of that strange melody which seemed sleeping in my soul. It has seldom happened, however, that I have owed such feelings to people; and no one ever gave me a moment of such happiness as it was my lot to feel one evening in the Church of Or San Michele, in Florence."

Seldom – *Rarely*
Disperse – *Break up*
Fiery – *Burning, Glowing*
Obscurity – *Uncertainty, Indistinctness*

"Tell me about it," said the Spirit.

"It was near sunset on a rainy spring afternoon in Easter week. The clouds had vanished, dispersed by a sudden wind, and as we entered the church the fiery panes of the high windows shone out like lamps through the dusk. A priest was at the high altar, his white cope a livid spot in the incense-laden obscurity, the light of the candles flickering up and down like fireflies about his head; a few people knelt near by. We stole behind them and sat down on a bench close to the tabernacle of Orcagna.

"Strange to say, though Florence was not new to me, I had never been in the church before; and in that magical light I saw for the first time the inlaid steps, the fluted columns, the sculptured bas-reliefs and canopy of the marvellous shrine.

The marble, worn and mellowed by the subtle hand of time, took on an unspeakable rosy hue, suggestive in some remote way of the honey-colored columns of the Parthenon, but more mystic, more complex, a color not born of the sun's inveterate kiss, but made up of cryptal twilight, and the flame of candles upon martyrs' tombs, and gleams of sunset through symbolic panes of chrysoprase and ruby; such a light as illumines the missals in the library of Siena, or burns like a hidden fire through the Madonna of Gian Bellini in the Church of the Redeemer, at Venice; the light of the Middle Ages, richer, more solemn, more significant than the limpid sunshine of Greece.

"The church was silent, but for the wail of the priest and the occasional scraping of a chair against the floor, and as I sat there, bathed in that light, absorbed in rapt contemplation of the marble miracle which rose before me, cunningly wrought as a casket of ivory and enriched with jewel-like incrustations and tarnished gleams of gold, I felt myself borne onward along a mighty current, whose source seemed to be in the very beginning of things, and whose tremendous waters gathered as they went all the mingled streams of human passion and endeavor.

Life in all its varied manifestations of beauty and strangeness seemed weaving a rhythmical dance around me as I moved, and wherever the spirit of man had passed I knew that my foot had once been familiar.

"As I gazed the medieval bosses of the tabernacle of Orcagna seemed to melt and flow into their primal forms

Wail – *Howl*
Rapt – *Absorbed*
Contemplation –
Deep thought
Antique – *Very old*

so that the folded lotus of the Nile and the Greek acanthus were braided with the runic knots and fish-tailed monsters of the North, and all the plastic terror and beauty born of man's hand from the Ganges to the Baltic quivered and mingled in Orcagna's apotheosis of Mary. And so the river bore me on, past the alien face of antique civilizations and the familiar wonders of Greece, till I swam upon the fiercely rushing tide of the Middle Ages, with its swirling eddies of passion, its heaven-reflecting pools of poetry and art; I heard the rhythmic blow of the craftsmen's hammers in the goldsmiths' workshops and on the walls of churches, the party-cries of armed factions in the narrow streets, the organ roll of Dante's verse, the crackle of the fagots around Arnold of Brescia, the twitter of the swallows to which St.

Francis preached, the laughter of the ladies listening on the hillside to the quips of the Decameron, while plague-struck Florence howled beneath them -- all this and much more I heard, joined in strange unison with voices earlier and more remote, fierce, passionate, or tender, yet subdued to such awful harmony that I thought of the song that the morning stars sang together and felt as though it were sounding in my ears.

My heart beat to suffocation, the tears burned my lids, the joy, the mystery of it seemed too intolerable to be borne. I could not understand even then the words of the song; but I knew that if there had been someone at my side who could have heard it with me, we might have found the key to it together.

"I turned to my husband, who was sitting beside me in an attitude of patient dejection, gazing into the bottom of his hat; but at that moment he rose, and stretching his stiffened legs, said, mildly: 'Hadn't we better be going? There doesn't seem to be much to see here, and you know the table d'hôte dinner is at half-past six o'clock."

Her recital ended, there was an interval of silence; then the Spirit of Life said, "There is a compensation in store for such needs as you have expressed."

"Oh, then you *do* understand?" she exclaimed. "Tell me what compensation, I entreat you!"

"It is ordained," the Spirit answered, "that every soul which seeks in vain on earth for a kindred soul to whom it

Harmony – *Agreement*
Entreat – *Beg*
Vain – *Hopeless*
Exultant – *Overjoyed*

can lay bare its inmost being shall find that soul here and be united to it for eternity."

A glad cry broke from her lips. "Ah, shall I find him at last?" she cried, exultant.

"He is here," said the Spirit of Life.

She looked up and saw that a man stood near whose soul (for in that unwonted light she seemed to see his soul more clearly than his face) drew her towards him with an invincible force.

"Are you really he?" she murmured.

"I am he," he answered.

She laid her hand in his and drew him toward the parapet which overhung the valley.

"Shall we go down together," she asked him, "into that marvellous country; shall we see it together, as if with the self-same eyes, and tell each other in the same words all that we think and feel?"

"So," he replied, "have I hoped and dreamed."

"What?" she asked, with rising joy. "Then you, too, have looked for me?"

"All my life."

"How wonderful! And did you never, never find anyone in the other world who understood you?" "Not wholly -- not as you and I understand each other."

"Then you feel it, too? Oh, I am happy," she sighed.

They stood, hand in hand, looking down over the para-pet upon the shimmering landscape which stretched forth beneath them into sapphirine space, and the Spirit of Life, who kept watch near the threshold, heard now and then a floating fragment of their talk blown backward like the stray swallows which the wind sometimes separates from their migratory tribe.

"Did you never feel at sunset --"

"Ah, yes; but I never heard anyone else say so. Did you?"

"Do you remember that line in the third canto of the 'Inferno?'"

"Ah, that line -- my favorite always. Is it possible --"

Marvellous –
Wonderful
Joy – *Happiness*
Threshold
– Doorstep

"You know the stooping Victory in the frieze of the Nike Apteros?"

"You mean the one who is tying her sandal? Then you have noticed, too, that all Botticelli and Mantegna are dormant in those flying folds of her drapery?"

"After a storm in autumn have you never seen --"

"Yes, it is curious how certain flowers suggest certain painters--the perfume of the incarnation, Leonardo; that of the rose, Titian; the tuberose, Crivelli --"

"I never supposed that anyone else had noticed it."

"Have you never thought --"

"Oh, yes, often and often; but I never dreamed that any-one else had."

"But surely you must have felt --"

"Oh, yes, yes; and you, too --"

"How beautiful! How strange --"

Their voices rose and fell, like the murmur of two fountains answering each other across a garden full of flowers. At length, with a certain tender impatience, he turned to her and said, "Love, why should we linger here? All eternity lies before us. Let us go down into that beautiful country together and make a home for ourselves on some blue hill above the shining river."

As he spoke, the hand she had forgotten in his was suddenly withdrawn, and he felt that a cloud was passing over the radiance of her soul.

"A home," she repeated, slowly, "a home for you and me to live in for all eternity?"

"Why not, love? Am I not the soul that yours has sought?"

"Y-yes -- yes, I know -- but, don't you see, home would not be like home to me, unless --"

"Unless?" he wonderingly repeated.

She did not answer, but she thought to herself, with an impulse of whimsical inconsistency, "Unless you slammed the door and wore creaking boots."

But he had recovered his hold upon her hand, and by imperceptible degrees was leading her toward the shining steps which descended to the valley.

Tender – *Caring*
Impulse – *Urge*
Whimsical
– *Unusual, Critical*

"Come, O my soul's soul," he passionately implored; "why delay a moment? Surely you feel, as I do, that eternity itself is too short to hold such bliss as ours. It seems to me that I can see our home already. Have I not always seem it in my dreams? It is white, love, is it not, with polished columns, and a sculptured cornice against the blue?

Groves of laurel and oleander and thickets of roses surround it; but from the terrace where we walk at sunset, the eye looks out over woodlands and cool meadows where, deep-bowered under ancient boughs, a stream goes delicately toward the river.

Indoors our favorite pictures hang upon the walls and the rooms are lined with books. Think, dear, at last we shall have time to read them all. With which shall we begin? Come, help me to choose. Shall it be 'Faust' or the 'Vita Nuova,' the 'Tempest' or 'Les Caprices de Marianne,' or the thirty-first canto of the 'Paradise,' or 'Epipsychidion' or "Lycidas'? Tell me, dear, which one?"

As he spoke he saw the answer trembling joyously upon her lips; but it died in the ensuing silence, and she stood motionless, resisting the persuasion of his hand.

"What is it?" he entreated.

"Wait a moment," she said, with a strange hesitation in her voice. "Tell me first, are you quite sure of yourself? Is there no one on earth whom you sometimes remember?"

"Not since I have seen you," he replied; for, being a man, he had indeed forgotten.

Still she stood motionless, and he saw that the shadow deepened on her soul.

"Surely, love," he rebuked her, "it was not that which troubled you? For my part I have walked through Lethe. The past has melted like a cloud before the moon. I never lived until I saw you."

She made no answer to his pleadings, but at length, rousing herself with a visible effort, she turned away from him and moved toward the Spirit of Life, who still stood near the threshold.

"I want to ask you a question," she said, in a troubled voice.

"Ask," said the Spirit.

Tremble – *Shiver*
Rebuke – *Scold*
Plead – *Beg*
Delusion – *Illusion*

"A little while ago," she began, slowly, "you told me that every soul which has not found a kindred soul on earth is destined to find one here."

"And have you not found one?" asked the Spirit.

"Yes; but will it be so with my husband's soul also?"

"No," answered the Spirit of Life, "for your husband imagined that he had found his soul's mate on earth in you; and for such delusions eternity itself contains no cure."

She gave a little cry. Was it of disappointment or triumph?

"Then -- then what will happen to him when he comes here?"

"That I cannot tell you. Some field of activity and happiness he will doubtless find, in due measure to his capacity for being active and happy."

She interrupted, almost angrily, "He will never be happy without me."

"Do not be too sure of that," said the Spirit.

She took no notice of this, and the Spirit continued, "He will not understand you here any better than he did on earth."

"No matter," she said; "I shall be the only sufferer, for he always thought that he understood me."

"His boots will creak just as much as ever --"

"No matter."

"And he will slam the door --"

"Very likely."

"And continue to read railway novels --"

She interposed, impatiently, "Many men do worse than that."

"But you said just now," said the Spirit, "that you did not love him."

"True," she answered, simply; "but don't you understand that I shouldn't feel at home without him? It is all very well for a week or two -- but for eternity!

After all, I never minded the creaking of his boots, except when my head ached, and I don't suppose it will ache *here*; and he was always so sorry when he had slammed the door, only he never *could* remember not to. Besides, no one else would know how to look after him, he is so helpless. His

Interpose – *Interject*
Abrupt – *Sudden*
Dismay –
Disappointment
Contemptuous –
Disapproving

inkstand would never be filled, and he would always be out of stamps and visiting cards.

He would never remember to have his umbrella re-covered, or to ask the price of anything before he bought it. Why, he wouldn't even know what novels to read. I always had to choose the kind he liked, with a murder or a forgery and a successful detective."

She turned abruptly to her kindred soul, who stood listening with a mien of wonder and dismay.

"Don't you see," she said, "that I can't possibly go with you?"

"But what do you intend to do?" asked the Spirit of Life.

"What do I intend to do?" she returned, indignantly. "Why, I mean to wait for my husband, of course. If he had come here first *he* would have waited for me for years and years; and it would break his heart not to find me here when he comes." She pointed with a contemptuous gesture to the magic vision of hill and vale sloping away to the translucent mountains. "He wouldn't give a fig for all that," she said, "if he didn't find me here."

"But consider," warned the Spirit, "that you are now choosing for eternity. It is a solemn moment." "Choosing!" she said, with a half-sad smile. "Do you still keep up here that old **fiction** about choosing? I should have thought that *you* knew better than that. How can I help myself? He will expect to find me here when he comes, and he would never believe you if you told him that I had gone away with someone else--never, never."

"So be it," said the Spirit. "Here, as on earth, each one must decide for himself."

She turned to her **kindred** soul and looked at him gently, almost **wistfully**. "I am sorry," she said. "I should have liked to talk with you again; but you will understand, I know, and I dare say you will find someone else a great deal cleverer --"

And without pausing to hear his answer she waved him a swift farewell and turned back towards the threshold.

Fiction
– Imagination, Unreal
Kindred *– Relatives*
Wistfully –
Thoughtfully

And still seated alone on the **threshold**, she listens for the creaking of his boots. "Will my husband come soon?" she asked the Spirit of Life.

"That you are not destined to know," the Spirit replied.

"No matter," she said, cheerfully; "I have all eternity to wait in."

Food For Thought

When the Spirit assured that every soul which seeks in vain on earth for a compatible soul finds one in heaven, then what was the reaction of the dying woman? Did her soul go with the soul of the man who drew her towards him with an invincible force? Why or why not? Think and Answer.

An Understanding

Q. 1. What do you think the story is all about? Why has the author, Edith Wharton name the story as 'The Fulness of Life'?

Ans. _____

_____

_____

_____

_____

Q. 2. "And so death is not the end after all." Why did the dying woman say this? She was having a conversation with whom?

Ans. _____

_____

_____

_____

_____

Q. 3. "You were married, yet you did not find the fulness of life in your marriage?" Who said this and why?

Ans. _____

_____

_____

_____

_____

Q. 4. In this story, the author writer that "a woman's life is like a great house full of rooms, most of which remain unseen, and in the innermost room, lies the Holy Soul which sits alone waiting endlessly for a footstep that never comes." What do you understand by these words? Why has the soul of a woman compared to the innermost room of a big house?

Ans. _____

_____

_____

_____

_____

Three Letters

~ Nels Schifano

IT 'was autumn. Although still afternoon the journey had been spent peering at slowly moving red lights through clouds of condensing exhaust and the intermittent slip-slip of wipers. Now as she turned off the ignition darkness gathered silently around her. She walked head down, hood up, feeling plastic handles moulding themselves around her fingers, the carrier bag spinning one way then the next as it clipped against her leg.

The pavement was thick with the slippery brown mulch of fallen leaves and the smell of bonfires wafted across the common. A thin mist clung around the streetlights producing a shifting yellow gas. Sounds were muffled and movements lethargic. Cars slipped slowly by on a film of dirty water. At her gate she delayed, unwilling to break the stillness with squeaking hinges; not yet tea time and the city was being put to sleep.

The terrace before her hugged the curve of the road tumbling erratically down the hill and into the gloom. Bending around the edges of her vision she was conscious of curtains being swished closed, stone faces bathed by the grey light of televisions, broken roof tiles, satellite dishes, bay windows, the whole higgledy-piggledy collection of guttering and skylights. For a moment her home was a stranger, a simple compartment in this huge connected structure.

She rattled the key into the lock, tilting it to the particular angle that would allow it to catch. She stepped inside, her hand brushing the light switch as she closed the door behind her. The softly lit warmth of the interior walls were a welcome contrast to the dark slimy surfaces of the outside. Two elderly neighbours warmed the house from the sides and soon she would hear the comforting noises of the boiler rousing itself into life.

She kept her mind occupied by these happy details of returning home as she walked along the hall and into the

Waft – *Float*
lethargic – *Tired, Lazy*
Gloom – *Darkness*
Contrast – *Difference*

kitchen. She lifted the carrier bag onto the worktop and reached for the kettle. Standing in the centre of the room, still in her anorak, she listened to the sound of the water boil and felt the house adjust itself to her presence. Now she returned at all times of the day she sometimes sensed she had caught it unawares. What ghosts that had been running through rooms were now slipping reluctantly back into walls? While its inhabitants had moved the house stayed still, preserving pockets of time in dusty corners. The blue-tak tears on bed-room walls, a water-colour sun and stick man hiding behind a fitted wardrobe, a dent in a table, a crack in a mirror, were all passing moments etched into the physical world, like voices pressed into vinyl.

Steam began to rise vertically to the ceiling where it changed direction aware of the presence of some subtle draft (or draft of some subtle presence). Through the window she could see the outline of the narrow garden, the fuzzy grey shapes of a rusting climbing frame and overflowing compost heap. Along one side a scruffy fence lent drunkenly one way then the other, while a brutally straight line of six-foot high boards marked the other side of the territory. What further anti-cat measures (minefields, tripwires perhaps) lay wait-ing beyond?

As if summoned by her thoughts Rahel, green eyes and a flicking tail, appeared on the window ledge, her si-lent meows making small circles of condensation. Smiling, she unlocked the door. The cat padded in, figures of eight around her feet represented by muddy paw prints on the kitchen floor. The kettle worked itself towards a crescendo, beads of perspiration appeared on its sides and it shook violently unable to contain the bubbling pressure inside. Abruptly it finished, sat back on the filament and turned itself off.

She reached up to the top cupboards for the coffee jar and bent down for those that contained the mugs. Here she paused, confused by the vast number of assorted cup, mugs, and beakers that stared blankly back at her. Why did she have so many? Where had they come from? She sighed as she straightened pulling out a standard shaped mug with

Reluctant
– Unwilling
Subtle *– Slight*
Scruffy *– Messy*
Territory *– Region*

handle; colour - light blue; design - three letters emblazoned in gold, S U E.

She took off her coat and laid it over the back of the oak kitchen chair and sat down. She let her feet slip out of her shoes and raised them onto the fitted bench across the other side of the table. Above the bench were shelves supporting decorative plates in wire stands, a Charles and Diana mug (more mugs!), and a collection of photographs showing either madly grinning or defiantly sulky children (both on the verge of crying). As she looked the image of a growing family seemed to slowly recede to reveal the image of a shrinking woman.

There was the sudden sound of water flooding into a drain as somewhere nearby a plug was pulled from a sink, a toilet was flushed or maybe a washing machine emptied itself and she realised that her coffee had gone cold. She moved to the sink and ran the hot water. Staring out into darkness she listened to the succession of far-off bangs and shudders from the network of pipes. Bathed in yellow light hovering over the gloom of the garden she looked in at a woman repeatedly working a tea towel around the inside of a mug. Who was she? Why was she so miserable?

She shook herself and took out the plug. Slipped away again into nothing time (that time that flowed into the gaps between the things you did). Wouldn't a wasted minute become a wasted hour, wasted hours become wasted days? Where could she be now if she hadn't been doing, what? Making tea, sitting in traffic jams, reading the local paper, standing in a supermarket queue? Best avoided, the thought of her life draining into these moments.

She unpacked the carrier bag. She put away the milk, the orange, the biscuits, and the cat food, then struggled to slide the two pizza's into an already crowded freezer spraying tiny shards of ice across the floor. An overflowing collection of polythene bags scrunched inside other polythene bags in the bottom of a cupboard was her commitment to recycling.

When it was opened a white plastic avalanche slid towards her. She threw in the latest addition and slammed the door. A lone bag made a break for freedom and buoyed by the

Defiant
– *Disobedient*
Recede – *Lessen*
Shudder – *Shake*
Miserable
– *Unhappy*
Lone – *Single*

swish of air it lifted across the room like a jellyfish. Two pairs of eyes followed its progress over the spice rack and bread-board until it was caught on a bottle of olive oil.

The oak bench was not just a foot rest. She had made this discovery during a rigorous cleaning session one New Year. Under the lip of the removable cushioned seat she had found a small catch, rusty enough to break two nails. Eventually it yielded and raised to reveal a dark, hollow chest.

Despite a few moments when her heartbeat seemed to fill the house, it proved to contain nothing more exciting than a pile of old newspapers - more dirtiness to clean. It was, she decided, an ideal place to store tablecloths and tea towels, but steadily it began to swallow bedding, pillow-cases and blankets of various sorts. Really, it was ridiculous to think that no one else was aware of its existence (was she the only one ever to change a bed, lay a table?) Still, she always thought of it as hers, and, when alone in the house, she opened it, she experienced a flush of childish excite-ment. She felt it rise now as her fingers fumbled beneath soft layers of folded cotton searching for the sharp cold of a shiny metal toffee tin.

She put the tin on the table. Inside lay a medal from the Polish Airforce; a commemorative coin; a pebble taken from Ilfracomb beach in 1978 (could she really remember the heavy heat of that day or did she need the proof of the pebble to tell her she had been there); a present bought but never given; and inside a neatly folded bag, three envelopes. She glanced around the room, from somewhere inside a wall a pipe clanked - the house clearing its throat - and took out the top envelope.

An antelope leapt across a colorful stamp. It looked startled as antelopes often do get caught in the sights of the black post-mark. The paper inside was thick and cream-coloured, it had a blue letterhead, and the date in the top right hand corner was July 2000. As she let her eyes wander over the page she noticed it was just a little crumpled, stiff in places, as if it had been wet-ted then dried.

Fumble – *Mistake*
Commemorative – *Remembrance*
Wander – *Stroll*
Reliable – *Dependable*

*

This must be something of a surprise. If, that is, this letter gets to you. I remembered your address, of course, but then it suddenly struck me that maybe you had moved and I didn't know and anyway the post round here isn't exactly reliable. So perhaps I am only writing a letter to myself.

Really now that I've started I can't think what it was I wanted to say. I think it was just the act of writing that was important, just to feel as if I was still in contact with things, although I guess a blank piece of paper in an envelope would have seemed a little strange.

I've really no need to ask how things are with you. It all seems to have worked out pretty much as you planned. But still I hope you are both healthy and happy.

I am afraid I've done nothing very exciting to tell you about. Here is just an endless succession of long boring tasks, and then there's the heat and the clouds of flies that rise from the river and make everything twice as hard. But this evening as I washed and dried my clothes suddenly there was this feeling of satisfaction. Strange, five months of toil and worry then calm descends as welcome and unexpected as an ice-cream van clattering through the bush.

Maybe that's why I am writing this letter. Perhaps it's thinking about England in the summer, perhaps it's the sounds of the river at night but my mind wandered back to the place of long afternoons, listening to Pink Moon and Lay Lady Lay. Can you still find a way back to the taste of cheap wine, the feel of grass between your fingers and a world that was all shimmering reflections?

All those people disappeared into the world. How would they be recognised now - perhaps only by the sound of their laughter?

Toil – *Work hard*
Carve – *Cut*
Respond – *Reply*
Silhouette – *The outline*

I'm afraid I once damaged the environment in your name and took a penknife to the willow we used to sit by. I can remember wondering if the bark would ever grow back. If you ever find yourself driving past one weekend . . . Well perhaps not, it's probably so sadly different. But I know your name will still be there, carved in the memory of a tree.

❋

She re-folded the letter and tapped it several times against her top lip. From the hall the clock calling out the quarter hour, then a moment of stillness - time stalling - before, faintly, the clock in her study responded.

She took out the next envelope. While her fingers searched for the flap she looked at the Queen's silver silhouette. The letter was written on paper so white and thin that as her gaze fell across it she saw it as a shade of blue. The date was April 1976.

❋

Do I remember that September afternoon when I first met you? Is it possible to remember the slide into sleep or the hypnotist's fingers on your eyelids? I only know that it happened because at some stage I awoke.

Some things are clear, the lucid fragments of a dream, a conversation over the phone one Easter. We both felt down because I was working in a stuffy shop and you in a sorting office. I hated it and asked you how it was that time moved so slowly. It's okay you said, it doesn't matter, because it will end and time passed is all the same, and anyway, in the end it's not time that you're left with.

You told me to go look for happiness and bring some back when I found it. But you can't bank happiness. You can't keep it for when you need it and you cannot give to someone else simply by having it yourself.

I thought I would be content to watch the river flow past and drift away on the scent of water lilies. I watched days become nights and nights gently give way to days, believing I was shedding my cares when really I was storing regrets. Now I know that reading is dreaming, that dreaming is sleeping and thought inaction. When I wake I find that all I have left is thoughts of you.

Lucid – *Clear*
Regrets – *Doubts*
Chase – *Run after*
Defer – *Postpone*
Serenity – *Calmness*

❋

The noise of the cat jumping clumsily onto her lap, the feeling of her pressing up and down with alternate paws, claws snagging loops of cotton.

This time the silhouette is not the Queen's but that of Nehru, a white head against an orange background. The stamp is stuck on at an odd angle (but still stuck after all this time!) and he stares down at the scraggly lines of a familiar address. The letter itself is written on a school child's lined paper, as her eyes run down the page they linger on the date, Nov. 1968 and the dappling of yellow blotches. What were they? Had they always been there?

*

I still can't believe you decided to go. Why go back to the grey, the dirt, the noise, the rush? There is a lifetime to do those things. I know you chase that dream of yours, but the dream is so sweetly deferred here. Here I feel as if I am absorbing the sunshine and serenity.

Since you left we moved further east where the earth here has a reddish tinge and so does the food. Today we met a group of Americans. We got a ride on the roof of their van and helped them collect firewood. They say there is an old man who sells the beads you wanted from the front of his hut, and eight miles of white sand.

I am writing this in a flickering of orange and blackness. This is the best time, talking and reading, the world melting away into words, although sometimes a phrase is so beautiful I have to walk around a little just to let them settle in. One of these made me think of you. 'Do that which makes you happy to do, and you will do right.'

*

The freezer's cooling mechanism rattled, then fell silent, and she realised that she hadn't been aware of the noise it was making. In its absence the air in the house seemed to hang with that same question; how would her life have been if she had managed to send just one of them? But the air received no answers and went back to its lazy circulation.

Lazy – *Lethargic*
Content – *Satisfied*

In time she would fold the letter away and place it back in the envelope, place the envelopes back into the bag, the bag back into the tin, and the tin into the trunk. She would cover it with layers of cloth and place down the seat and lock the catch. But now she just sat for a moment, the noise of the cat's contented breathing filling the house.

Food For Thought

The old woman had a lover who was in Polish Airforce. She wrote 'three letters', but never posted them as she was not sure where her lover was. She was now remembering her old days - the love that started in one September afternoon, when she first met her lover. Can you tell what would have been the woman's life if she had managed to send just one of the letters?

An Understanding

Q. 1. Why did the author, Nels Schifano chose an Autumn afternoon to begin the story? What is the story all about in brief?
Ans. _____

_____
_____
_____
_____

Q. 2. Where did the old woman stay? What does the description suggest? Was she old, weak, tired and alone?
Ans. _____

_____
_____
_____
_____

Q. 3. What had she bought from the market? What was she preparing for herself?
Ans. _____

_____
_____
_____
_____

Q. 4. What had she kept inside a shiny metal toffee tin? Why did she write the letters to her lover and never posted them? Why did she buy a gift but never gave him?
Ans. _____

_____
_____
_____
_____

Highway Time

~ Jennifer Jenkinson

THe big older Pontiac sped along eating up mile upon mile of highway. The driver slouched indolently behind the wheel, his left elbow resting comfortably on the car window fingers steadying the wheel but not gripping it, tapping in time to the classic rock on the radio. His right hand gripped the wheel at almost the top, but even that grip was relaxed, almost lazy. His rich hazel eyes were hidden behind aviator style sunglasses. He had a strong chin with a neatly trimmed goatee which matched his equally neatly trimmed short black hair.

The highway he was on stretched the length of the country, The Trans-Canada Highway, and he was driving west from the prairies towards the West Coast. The Rocky Mountains stretched before him, running north to south, like an impenetrable barrier. But Evan Kirby knew better; the highway found its winding way through mountain passes across the continental divide over several ranges ending in the Pacific Coastal Range and the sea.

There by the sea, on the great Fraser River Delta which two million or more souls called home, lay Vancouver, a port city, a crossroads of the world. But the draw there for Evan was the rich and bountiful entertainment industry. Evan Kirby was a guitar player. He had played with an assortment of bands in prairie towns and cities but, drawn to classic rock and the new innovative sounds coming out of some of the west coast studios, had decided to try his luck in Vancouver. After all, he had reasoned, the weather's warmer there too.

The car was a cluttered mess and a Marshall amplifier took up more than half of the back seat. Some fast food bags and beverage cups littered the floor. On the seat beside him was a Calgary newspaper, a copy of Guitarplayer Magazine and a couple of CD's. As the car cruised further into the mountains the Calgary radio station he had been listening to started to crackle and break up. Evan steadied the wheel with a couple of fingers only and loaded a CD into the player. The car was

Indolently – *Lazily*
Barrier – *Obstacle*
Bountiful – *Plentiful*
Clutter – *Mess*

filled with the sound of Led Zepplin as he cruised through the Banff National Park Gates.

Just west of the Banff townsite there were a couple of hitchhikers along the road. The first two were a grubby looking pair of men which Evan barely looked at. But his eyes were drawn to the slim girlish figure standing alone clutching a small pack to her side almost as though it were a teddy bear. The wind was blowing her long straight blonde hair wildly from beneath her hat, a crocheted close-fitting soft turquoise cap.

She wore a pair of flared, faded, and somewhat tattered blue jeans and a shirt that was a tight fitting long sleeved soft knit fabric in a darker turquoise than her hat with a dragon boldly painted across the front. Evan whistled under his breath as he pulled over to pick her up. 'Geez, she's just a kid.' he thought, 'They just get younger.'

She seemed to struggle to pull open the passenger door and he was again struck by how young and fragile she looked. She put her bag on the seat between them and managed a shy smile at him before her eyes slid self-consciously to her hands in her lap. "Thanks," she said in a near whisper.

Evan put the car back into gear and glanced over his shoulder before accelerating back onto the highway. He glanced sidelong at his passenger, wondering what she was running away from. "How far you going?" he asked.

"Vancouver." she murmured softly, still only one word.

Evan chuckled lightly to himself. "Great," he told her, "I'm headed there too, you're in luck."

"Thanks," she whispered again.

Evan concentrated more on his driving now as the road wound its way through some of the most spectacular scenery on the continent, the highway clung to mountainsides and traversed canyons and wound through rocky valley floors. He cast occasional surreptitious looks at the girl beside him. She, for her part, was absolutely silent but her eyes watched the passing scenery with something akin to reverence.

The Led Zepplin CD ended and Evan reached for the other case on the seat beside him. He held it out towards the girl and she looked at him with a question in her eyes.

Grubby – *Dirty*
Tatter – *Scrap*
Fragile – *Delicate*
Murmur – *Speak softly*
akin – *Similar*

"Put that on will ya." he said with a grin. She glanced at the CD and smiled shyly. She fumbled a bit with the CD player but managed to get Evan's CD in. The sounds of Treble Charger filled the car. Though he was still watching the road, he smiled as he noticed that she was tapping her feet in time to the music.

"You like?" he asked.

"Yeah," she said softly, another one-word answer.

"Cool." he replied. "They're pretty good, they rock, ya know? By the way, I'm Evan."

She glanced briefly at him and lapsed into silence, her eyes again falling to study the papers and magazines between them. When a few moments went by without a word from her, Evan tried again.

"I'm Evan." he repeated softly, "What's your name, kid?"

Her fingers brushed the magazine cover nervously before she finally spoke, "I'm Sky," she answered, "and I'm not a kid."

He gripped the steering wheel a little tighter as the big car negotiated an especially tight turn with a dizzying drop off on his left, but all the same he'd noticed her fingers had passed over a headline which read The Sky is Crying - SRV Gone Ten Years as she had found a voice to introduce herself. He smiled to himself.

"Okay Sky, pleased to meet you." he told her. "So what takes you to Vancouver?"

"You do." she said, with a sarcastic tone.

Evan laughed deeply and heartily. She had spirit and spunk for sure, he thought, maybe after all she was old enough to be out on the road. She laughed nervously too as though relieved he had not become angry at her sarcasm.

The car sped on eating up miles of road. Past Field, BC as they had passed from Alberta to the most western province and through Golden. As they continued through the valley between one mountain range and the next towards Revelstoke, Evan began to feel hungry and tired. 'Time for a break,' he thought, then almost guiltily he wondered how long it had been since Sky had eaten.

Negotiate – *Discuss*
Sarcastic – *Ironic*
Relieve – *Ease*
cling – *Stick*

"We'll be in Revelstoke in about twenty minutes," he told her, "I need to get gas, and I'm gonna grab a bite, okay?"

"Okay," she said, still watching the ever changing scenery as they sped along.

When he slid from the car at the gas station she clung to her backpack and watched him with something akin to fear in her eyes. He wondered again just what she was running from or perhaps it was running to. He made a half-hearted effort to clean the highway dust and squished bugs off the windshield and when he started on her side of the glass he waved and winked at her through the window and was pleased when she relaxed a little and stuck out her tongue at him.

He pulled into a twenty-four hour highway diner just down the strip from the gas station and slid out of the car once more. Sky hesitated. Evan leaned his six foot frame over to peer across the seat at her. "You coming?" he asked.

She got out, still carrying her pack and followed him into the diner, her shorter legs moving almost at a run to keep pace with his long lazy strides. They were shown to a booth in a quiet corner of the almost empty diner and the hostess poured Evan a mug of coffee then left to get the glass of cola that Sky had requested. Evan stirred a couple of large spoons of sugar into his black coffee and glanced through the menu. He watched as Sky didn't offer to open her menu but instead idly toyed with the cutlery and paper napkin. The hostess returned with the cola and Sky thanked her softly.

"You're welcome hon," the hostess said, then turned towards Evan. "Your server will be with you in a moment."

He smiled up at her and nodded his thanks. As she walked away he took a long swallow of the coffee. "Man, I needed that." he chuckled. Sky smiled shyly at him and took a tiny sip from her cola, as though trying to make it last a long time. He stretched his legs comfortably beneath the table and leaned back lazily in the booth.

"Better eat now," he told her. "I'm not planning on stopping except for gas between here and the coast, it's gonna be a long night."

She shifted uncomfortably under his gaze and toyed with her straw. He was about to say more but decided against further comment as the waitress approached with a pad in hand. He guessed, correctly, that she did not have enough money

Peer – *Stare*
Glance – *Quick look*
Chuckle – *Laugh to yourself*
Afford – *Have enough money*
Wry – *Ironic*

to afford eating. 'I'm a sucker,' he thought wryly, 'But what the hell.'

"Are you ready to order?" the young woman with the pad asked with a tired smile.

"Yeah thanks," Ewan said. "We'll have two cheeseburgers deluxe, with gravy for the fries."

"Alright Sir, thank you." she said, scribbling quickly and picking up the menus. Sky stared open mouthed at him as the waitress moved away. He grinned at her in mock shock.

"What? You do eat, don't you?" he asked.

"Evan, I can't pay for this." she told him. "I'm kind of broke, you know?"

"Yeah, I kind of guessed, Sky." he answered her. "It's my treat okay? No strings, don't worry. You look like you could use a meal."

"Thank you," she murmured. She took another sip of her cola and lowered her face away from his again. He watched her hand as her fingertips brushed across her eyes and came away shiny with her liquid tears. 'She's crying.' he marvelled. He stifled his first instinct to comfort her and instead changed the subject.

"Glad you like Treble Charger," he said. "There's a lotta cool stuff happening in music these days. I'm kinda hoping I can get in with some players in Vancouver and get a regular studio gig, ya know?"

"You're a musician?" she asked.

"Yeah, guitar player." he said "Figure I'll get some work out there pretty easy. How 'bout you?"

She took another drink from her cola before replying. "I'm going to join my boyfriend."

He considered that for a moment, wondering if her parents knew she had up and run after some guy, and also, if the guy had any idea she was on the way to join him. He drained his coffee and caught the waitress with just a quick nod and smile for a refill. As he sweetened the coffee once more, he tried to draw her out more.

"That's cool Sky." he smiled. "Bet he's happy you're gonna join him. Musta been hard to be so far apart, huh?"

Marvel – *Wonder*
Stifle – *Suffocate*
Audible – *Capable of being heard*
Convince – *Persuade*

The waitress came back with their cheeseburgers and Sky was silent until she had left again. Then, as she took her first bite of the burger, she mumbled a barely audible answer.

"He don't know I'm coming exactly. But he'll be happy to see me, I just know it."

Evan got the impression she was trying to convince herself. He took her lead and started on his own burger, letting the conversation slide for a while. In the light and face to face like this, Evan guessed she could not be more than half his age, fifteen maybe sixteen. After getting half way through his meal in silence, he took a long swallow of ice water and let his curiosity find voice again.

"So, your boyfriend," he began tentatively, "He go out to Van for work too?"

She eyed him as though she were considering one of those sarcastic answers, but his soft hazel eyes met hers with nothing more than kindness and concern. She dipped a fry into the gravy and watched the gravy drip from it onto her plate as she spoke. "I don't know. He just split, ya know?"

Evan nodded, "Yeah I remember what that was like. When I was sixteen, I just split. Couldn't handle my parents and teachers telling me what to do anymore. And there was this chick, well ya know, she thought we was getting married or something. And hell, I was only sixteen. So I just split." He reached for the other half of his burger, concentrating on the food once again and letting his words sink in.

She ate her fries in silence for a while, her free hand nervously playing with a long strand of her blonde hair. Finally, she took a deep breath and looked away from him, out the window as she spoke, "It wasn't like that. He's just confused and scared is all. He'll be so happy when I get there. It'll be okay. After all, he's gonna be a daddy."

"Damn!" Evan exclaimed, all pretense of deference gone as his shock was obvious. Sky moved uneasily in her seat, taking a hold of her backpack as though she was going to simply run. He quickly recovered some of his dispassionate tone and added with a kind smile, "Congratulations that's awesome. Eat up girl, you're eating for two." The waitress came by just then and refilled Evan's coffee mug for the third time.

Tentatively – *Shyly*
Pretence – *Make-believe*
deference – *Respect*
interrupt – *Break off*

She took Sky's now empty cola glass and asked her if she wanted more. He quickly interrupted and ordered a glass of milk for the girl before she could speak. Sky at first looked angrily at him but her face softened to a shy smile before she spoke.

"Thank you, Evan." she said. "That would be good for the baby. Ryan would take care of me like that, ya know?"

"Sure kid," Evan agreed, half heartedly. She did not protest his choice of words. They both silently went back to eating.

Sky finished before him and excused herself to find the ladies room. He was surprised that she left her pack with him at the table. 'Perhaps a gesture of trust.' he thought. As he finished his fries between sips of the strong black coffee, he wondered what sort of home she had left behind and whether she had even considered how she would bring a child up on the cruel streets of a big city like Vancouver. His logic told him that she should be going home, certainly her parents must be worried and, like any parents, though they would be upset with her situation, they would help her. Sky's own assessment of her boyfriend was probably quite correct too, he thought, the kid had run because he was scared. Evan doubted that Sky's sudden appearance in Vancouver would change that any.

She returned to the table just as he gulped down the last of his coffee. He grinned at her, as he stood up, "Finish your milk, I'm just gonna recycle this coffee. Then we'll get on the road." She smiled gratefully up at him and took the milk glass in both hands as he turned away.

When they got back to the car, he unlocked her door first and held it for her as she settled herself back on the wide front seat. He opened the trunk and pulled a blanket out. When he got into the car, he draped the blanket across the back of the long front seat. He noticed she was no longer clinging to her back pack but had left it on the seat between them. He motioned to the glove compartment in front of her.

"There's some more CD's in there." You're in charge of music, okay?"

Draped – *Dress*
Indistinct – *Unclear*
urge – *Insist on*

"Okay." she giggled and quickly retrieved the small stack of CD's. As he started the car and headed along the service road back to the main highway, she was going through each CD, examining the covers. She finally selected Red Hot Chili Peppers just as Evan put his foot down and accelerated west again along the highway.

Evan relaxed into his comfortable driving posture as the big car ate up the miles. Beside him, Sky continued to watch the scenery go by but as the sun was setting quickly ahead of them the once sharp images were becoming indistinct and the mountain peaks, once towering majestically over the road, began to blend into the darkening sky behind them. Evan tapped his hands in time to the music and resisted the urge to draw the girl into further conversation. More than a half an hour had passed when she finally broke the silence between them. "Evan?" she asked tentatively.

"Yah." he drawled lazily.

"If you were sixteen and your girl got pregnant, you'd be pretty scared, huh?" she asked softly.

Evan's fingers briefly stopped their rhythmic tapping. "Yeah baby, I'da been scared shitless."

"I know Ryan was scared." she conceded. "But he tried to hide it, you know? Like he was all mad at me and all. Then I heard from some of the kids that he'd split for the coast. And I got all scared too, you know? Like maybe he was just mad at me."

Evan took a deep even breath before he answered her. "It's a scary thing for both of you, Sky. That's a new life, a new person growing inside of you now."

"Yeah, I know," she murmured. "I don't know if Ryan can handle that, you know? We haven't known each other long. Like we met at the roller rink where a lotta the kids hang out. And he was so great, you know. And my girlfriends said, 'Like go for it, he's so good looking.' Then he invited me to go to this party and, well, you know. . . . ." her voice trailed off.

Evan was struck by the irony that she couldn't bring herself to tell him that she had gone to bed with this so-called boyfriend but now found herself carrying his child. He made no comment, waiting for her to continue. When she spoke again, her voice was choked with emotion and unshed tears. "Now I've just gotta find him, you know? I can't do this alone. Damn, I'm so scared."

Conceded – *Approved*
Sob – *Cry*

Evan glanced sidelong at her, noting her hands were clutched tightly together in her lap. The expected tears didn't come but her face turned away from him and she stared out into the growing darkness. Evan spoke, without taking his eyes from the highway, "Sky, you have every right to be scared. But you gotta let that fear work for ya, baby. You've got a baby coming now and that baby needs you. What's best for your baby, Sky? Running to Vancouver, where you might find this Ryan guy and he might help you or not. That don't sound too good for you or your baby, ya know?"

"I know." she whispered, then sobbed almost desperately, "But I can't go home now! Mom and Dad, don't even know I'm pregnant. They'd kill me." When her tears came, they were silent.

Again Evan resisted his first urge to comfort her. 'God.' he thought, 'You're in way too deep here Evan, this is a kid, having a baby!' He drove in silence as she cried herself out. Finally when she calmed a bit he spoke again.

"Sky, I don't think you're giving your parents enough credit. After all, girl, they raised you. And look at all the courage and smarts you've got. To be out here at all took guts, girl. Maybe you should think about telling them where you are, you know. And what's been going on. Then just see what happens. You can call when we get down close to Vancouver, then if you don't hear what you want, you don't have to do anything about it. Just go on and look for Ryan. That's if you still think he wants to be found."

She was silent for so long that Evan was unsure if he'd gone too far. Finally, she sniffled a couple of times and turned from the darkness towards him. "You really think it'd be okay? My parents, I mean." she asked.

"Yeah baby," he assured her. "They'll be upset, of course, but it'll be fine."

"I'll think about it, Evan. "Cause Ryan, ya know, he's too scared I think," she said into a silence made more profound by the fact that the CD had just ended. Evan smiled in the darkness.

Sky changed the CD again, sliding Goo Goo Dolls into the player. Shortly after that, Evan noted that she had slipped into

Courage – *Bravery*
Unsure – *Uncertain*
Sniffle – *Sob*
Profound – *Deep*

a far more relaxed posture. Within a couple of miles, she had slumped over onto her backpack which made a good pillow. He reached behind him and pulled the blanket down from the back of the seat, spreading it across her sleeping form as best he could. Evan hummed to himself as the big Pontiac continued eat up the miles, winding down through the Fraser Canyon towards the coast.

Hours later, as Evan decelerated into a service road in Abbotsford, Sky stirred beside him. She yawned, stretched, and rubbed the sleep from her eyes. When she sat upright, he saw her glancing around, trying to get some bearings, the post midnight darkness combined with the nearby brightness of street and neon lighting completely hid any landmarks from view and Evan wondered if she would have recognized them in any case.

"We're in Abbotsford, sleepyhead," he told her. "Almost there. Thought I'd stop for a coffee and maybe if you still wanna make that call. . . ." he trailed off, leaving the thought unfinished.

"Umm Evan, I'd have to call collect," she said softly. "I really didn't bring much with me."

He pulled in to an all night diner parking lot and parked next to the building where a neon blue strip lit up a pay phone. He turned to face her, reaching across the back seat for his jacket as he spoke, "So call collect. I'm betting they won't mind much about a few bucks for a phone call, just so they know their girl's okay, ya know?" Without waiting for her response, he slid from the car and she watched his retreating form enter the diner.

When he returned with a large styrofoam coffee cup in his hand, she was standing shivering in front of the phone. Evan put the coffee onto the roof of the big Pontiac and grabbed the blanket from the front seat. She looked sidelong at him as he draped it round her shoulders and her hesitant fingers picked up the receiver.

He stepped a respectful distance away as she placed the call, picking up the coffee, and staring into the darkness. It took a few moments for the operator to connect the call and she looked up at him with fear in her pretty eyes. He gave her what he hoped was a reassuring smile and a thumbs up from

Retreating – *Moving back*

Reassuring – *Comforting*

Dismay – *Disappointment*

the hand not holding the coffee. Then her full attention went to the phone and he knew he had gambled right and her parents had accepted the call.

"Daddy," she said uncertainly. Then, "Daddy I'm okay. I'm in Abbotsford." Another pause and then, "I hitchhiked, I was looking for Ryan." She listened a long time and cast a tear-filled glance at Evan. He nodded as positively as he could at her. At last she spoke again, her voice shaking, "Daddy I have something to tell you . . ." a short pause, then her words came in a sobbing rush, "I'm pregnant.

That's why I was looking for Ryan. And then Evan gave me a ride and he said I should call you, and I . . ." She looked directly at Evan now, tears streaming again, but listening still. Finally she spoke again, "Evan is a guitar player, he's going to work in recording studios in Vancouver, he . . . No Daddy he's really been nice, he said to talk to you. Daddy, I wanna come home," she finished plaintively. She listened for a long time then, without warning, thrust the receiver towards Evan. At first he shook his head in dismay, then he relented and took the phone.

"Hello?" he said hesitantly.

The voice on the other end was firm but not angry. "I understand you picked up my daughter, Evan? That's right isn't it? Evan?"

"Yes Sir, my name is Evan Kirby," he said keeping his voice even and calm. "She kinda looked like she needed a friend. I'm a sucker for strays, ya know?"

"Seems to me, young man, I owe you," the other man said, "Meredith was lucky that it was you that picked her up and convinced her to make this call."

Evan had looked in some surprise at Sky when her father had mentioned her real name. The girl would always be Sky in his mind. "She convinced herself, Sir. I just listened, ya know?"

"Donít call me Sir, Evan. The name's Geoff Cavanaugh," Meredith's father told him. "I have a last favour to ask of you, if you could see your way clear to drive my girl to the Vancouver Airport? I'll see that a ticket home is waiting there for her."

Calm – *Peaceful*
owe – *Be obliged*
Somtre – *Serious*
Companion
– *Friend*

"Yeah Mr. Cavanaugh, it'd be a pleasure," he replied.

"Thank you, Mr. Kirby. I won't ever forget what you did for her."

Neither Evan nor Sky spoke for much of the rest of the drive into Vancouver. It was starting to get light and the city was grey and somewhat somber under early morning cloud cover. Evan tuned the radio in to a local Vancouver classic rock station. Beside him, Sky gazed around at everything as though trying to memorize it; her first ever view of Vancouver. He rapidly located the route through the city to the southside and the International Airport.

"You don't have to come inside with me," she told him half-heartedly.

Evan chuckled at her. "Of course I do, baby. Completes the circle, ya know?" He parked the car, pocketed the key, and walked beside her to the terminal.

She picked up the ticket which her father had left for her. With Evan protectively beside her, they found their way towards the departures hallway. She stopped just short of the security clearance area and looked up at her tall travelling companion. Tears filled her eyes once more.

"Evan, thank you," she whispered, solemnly sticking out her small hand to shake his larger one. He winked at her and, instead of taking her hand, opened both his arms and wrapped the slim girl in a warm big brotherly hug.

"Thank you, sweet Sky," he crooned at her. "Take care of yourself, kiddo. And take care of your baby, okay?"

He stepped back and she turned towards the gate. She looked back over her shoulder, smiling through her tears, "Good bye Evan," she called, "I'll look for you on MTV."

He grinned at her, blew her a kiss and called back. "If it's a boy, Evan's a good strong name, ya know?"

She turned and was gone.

Thirty minutes later, Evan Kirby sat in front of the viewing lounge windows in Vancouver International Airport and watched the 767 lift into the sky heading east. He took and

Grin – *Smile*
Ineffectually – *Weakly*

long drink of yet another sweet black coffee and ineffectually wiped a tear from the corner of his eye. He arose, leaving the rest of his coffee where it sat, and strode quickly towards the exit doors.

Food For Thought

Why, do you think that the girl's boyfriend was angry with her? Why did the girl ask Evan that if he were sixteen and his girl got pregnant, would he be scared? Did Evan give the right advice to the girl? If yes, why? If no, then why?

An Understanding

Q. 1. Give a brief character sketch of Evan Kirby? How old was he?

Ans. _____

_____

_____

_____

_____

Q. 2. What was Evan's profession? Whom did he give lift to on his way to Vancouver?

Ans. _____

_____

_____

_____

_____

Q. 3. How did Evan get to know the young girl? How old was she and why did she run away from her home?

Ans. _____

_____

_____

_____

_____

Q. 4. How did Evan convince the girl to call her parents? Why did he think that her boyfriend, Ryan would not take care of her even in Vancouver?

Ans. _____

_____

_____

_____

_____

O. Henry

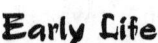

Born on September 11, 1862
Died on June 5, 1910
Pen name: O. Henry, or Oliver Henry
Notable Works: *The Gift of the Magi, The Ransom of Red Chief, The Cop and the Anthem, A Retrieved Reformation, The Duplicity of Hargraves, The Last Leaf, etc.*

Early Life

William Sydney Porter, popularly known by his pen name, **O. Henry**, was born on September 11, 1862 in Greensboro, North Carolina. He was one of the most popular American writers well-known for his short stories, which are full of wit, wordplay, warm characterisation and clever twist endings. His parents were Dr. Algernon Sidney Porter, a physician, and Mary Jane Virginia Swaim Porter. As a child, Porter was always reading, everything from classics to dime novels. Porter graduated from his aunt Evelina Maria Porter's elementary school in 1876. He then enrolled at the Lindsey Street High School. His aunt continued to tutor him until he was fifteen. In 1879, he started working in his uncle's drugstore and in 1881, at the age of nineteen, he was licensed as a pharmacist. At the drugstore, he also showed off his natural artistic talents by sketching the townsfolk.

He then worked full time on his humorous weekly called *The Rolling Stone*, which he started while working at the bank. *The Rolling Stone* featured satire on life, people and politics and included Porter's short stories and sketches. Although eventually, reaching a top circulation of 1500, *The Rolling Stone* failed in April 1895, since the paper never provided an adequate income. However, his writings and drawings had caught the attention of the editor at the Houston Post. Porter and his family moved to Houston in 1895, where he started writing for the *Post*. Porter gathered ideas for his column by loitering in hotel lobbies and observing and talking to people there. This was a technique he used throughout his writing career.

Literary Works and Achievements

Cabbages and Kings was his first collection of stories, followed by *The Four Million*. Among his most famous stories are: *The Gift of the Magi* about a young couple, who are short of money but desperately want to buy each other Christmas gifts; *The Ransom of Red Chief*, in which two men kidnap a boy of ten. The boy turns out to be so bratty and obnoxious that the desperate men ultimately pay the boy's father $250 to take him back, *The Cop and the Anthem*, *A Retrieved Reformation*, *The Duplicity of Hargraves, The Last Leaf* and many more.

Writing Style

O. Henry's stories frequently have surprise endings. In his day, he was called the American answer to Guy de Maupassant. Both authors wrote plot twist endings, but O. Henry stories were much more playful. His stories are also known for witty narration. Most of O. Henry's stories are set in his own time, the early 20th century. Many take place in New York City and deal for the most part with ordinary people: clerks, policemen, waitresses, etc.

Later Years

Porter's or O. Henry's most prolific writing period started in 1902, when he moved to New York City to be near his publishers. While there, he wrote about **381 short stories**. He wrote a story a week for over a year for the *New York World Sunday Magazine*. His wit, characterisation, and plot twists were adored by his readers, but often panned by critics.

Porter was a heavy drinker, and his health deteriorated markedly in 1908, which affected his writing. In 1909, his wife, Sarah left him, and he died on June 5, 1910, of cirrhosis of the liver, complications of diabetes, and an enlarged heart. After funeral services in New York City, he was buried in the Riverside Cemetery in Asheville, North Carolina. His daughter, Margaret Worth Porter, who died in 1927, was buried next to her father.

Trivia

The **O. Henry Award** is a prestigious annual prize named after Porter and given to outstanding short stories of the world. Several schools around United States bear Porter's pseudonym.

Past One At Rodney's

~ O. Henry

ONly on the lower East Side of New York do the houses of Capulet and Montagu survive. There they do not fight by the book of arithmetic. If you but bite your thumb at an upholder of your opposing house you have work cut out for your steel. On Broadway you may drag your man along a dozen blocks by his nose, and he will only bawl for the watch; but in the domain of the East Side Tybalts and Mercutios you must observe the niceties of deportment to the wink of any eyelash and to an inch of elbow room at the bar when its patrons include foes of your house and kin.

So, when Eddie McManus, known to the Capulets as Cork McManus, drifted into Dutch Mike's for a stein of beer, and came upon a bunch of Montagus making merry with the suds, he began to observe the strictest parliamentary rules. Courtesy forbade his leaving the saloon with his thirst unslaked; caution steered him to a place at the bar where the mirror supplied the cognizance of the enemy's movements that his indifferent gaze seemed to disdain; experience whispered to him that the finger of trouble would be busy among the chattering steins at Dutch Mike's that night. Close by his side drew Brick Cleary, his Mercutio, companion of his perambulations. Thus they stood, four of the Mulberry Hill Gang and two for the Dry Dock Gang, minding their P's and Q's so solicitously that Dutch Mike kept one eye on his customers and the other on an open space beneath his bar in which it was his custom to seek safety whenever the ominous politeness of the rival associations congealed into the shapes of bullets and cold steel.

But we have not to do with the wars of the Mulberry Hills and the Dry Docks. We must to Rooney's, where, on the most blighted dead branch of the tree of life, a little pale orchid shall bloom. Overstrained etiquette at last gave way. It is not known who first overstepped the bounds of punctilio; but the consequences were immediate. Buck Malone, of the Mulberry Hills, with a Dewey-like swiftness, got an eight-inch gun swung round from his hurricane deck. But McManus's simile must be the torpedo. He glided in under the guns and slipped a scant three inches of knife blade between the ribs of the

Bawl – *Howl, wail*
Foe – *Enemy*
Courtesy – *Good manners*
Disdain – *Contempt*

Mulberry Hill cruiser. Meanwhile Brick Cleary, a devotee to strategy, had skimmed across the lunch counter and thrown the switch of the electrics, leaving the combat to be waged by the light of gunfire alone. Dutch Mike crawled from his haven and ran into the street crying for the watch instead of for a Shakespeare to immortalize the Cimmerian shindy.

The cop came, and found a prostrate, bleeding Montagu supported by three distrait and reticent followers of the House. Faithful to the ethics of the gangs, no one knew whence the hurt came. There was no Capulet to be seen.

"Raus mit der interrogatories," said Buck Malone to the officer. "Sure I know who done it. I always manage to get a bird's eye view of any guy that comes up an' makes a show case for a hardware store out of me. No. I'm not telling you his name. I'll settle with um meself. Wow - ouch! Easy, boys! Yes, I'll attend to his case meself. I'm not making any complaint."

At midnight McManus strolled around a pile of lumber near an East Side dock, and lingered in the vicinity of a certain water plug. Brick Cleary drifted casually to the trysting place ten minutes later. "He'll maybe not croak," said Brick; "and he won't tell, of course. But Dutch Mike did. He told the police he was tired of having his place shot up. It's unhandy just now, because Tim Corrigan's in Europe for a week's end with Kings. He'll be back on the *Kaiser Williams* next Friday. You'll have to duck out of sight till then. Tim'll fix it up all right for us when he comes back."

This goes to explain why Cork McManus went into Rooney's one night and there looked upon the bright, stranger face of Romance for the first time in his precarious career.

Until Tim Corrigan should return from his jaunt among Kings and Princes and hold up his big white finger in private offices, it was unsafe for Cork in any of the old haunts of his gang. So he lay, perdu, in the high rear room of a Capulet, reading pink sporting sheets and cursing the slow paddle wheels of the *Kaiser Wilhelm*.

It was on Thursday evening that Cork's seclusion became intolerable to him. Never a hart panted for water fountain as he did for the cool touch of a drifting stein, for the firm security of a foot-rail in the hollow of his shoe and the quiet, hearty challenges of friendship, and repartee along and across the shining bars. But he must avoid the district where he was known. The

Ominous –
Threatening,
Inauspicious
Combat – *Battle*
Reticent – *Quiet*
Jaunt – *Outing*
Seclusion – *Privacy*

cops were looking for him everywhere, for news was scarce, and the newspapers were harping again on the failure of the police to suppress the gangs. If they got him before Corrigan came back, the big white finger could not be uplifted; it would be too late then. But Corrigan would be home the next day, so he felt sure there would be small danger in a little excursion that night among the crass pleasures that represented life to him.

At half-past twelve McManus stood in a darkish cross-town street looking up at the name "Rooney's," picked out by incandescent lights against a signboard over a second-story window. He had heard of the place as a tough "hang-out"; with its frequenters and its locality he was unfamiliar. Guided by certain unerring indications common to all such resorts, he ascended the stairs and entered the large room over the cafe.

Here were some twenty or thirty tables, at this time about half-filled with Rooney's guests. Waiters served drinks. At one end a human pianola with drugged eyes hammered the keys with automatic and furious unprecision. At merciful intervals a waiter would roar or squeak a song - songs full of "Mr. Jonsons" and "babes" and "coons" - historical word guaranties of the genuineness of African melodies composed by red waist-coated young gentlemen, natives of the cotton fields, and rice swamps of West Twenty-eighth Street.

For one brief moment you must admire Rooney with me as he receives, seats, manipulates, and chaffs his guests. He is twenty-nine. He has Wellington's nose, Dante's chin, the cheek-bones of an Iroquois, the smile of Talleyrand, Corbett's foot work, and the pose of an eleven-year-old East Side Central Park Queen of the May. He is assisted by a lieutenant known as Frank, a pudgy, easy chap, swell-dressed, who goes among the tables seeing that dull care does not intrude. Now, what is there about Rooney's to inspire all this pother? It is more respectable by daylight; stout ladies with children and mittens and bundles and unpedigreed dogs drop up of afternoons for a stein and a chat. Even by gaslight the diversions are melancholy in the mouth - drink and rag-time, and an occasional surprise when the waiter swabs the suds from under your sticky glass. There is an answer. Transmigration! The soul of Sir Walter Raleigh has traveled from beneath his slashed doublet to a kindred home under Rooney's visible plaid waistcoat. Rooney's is twenty years ahead of the times. Rooney has removed the embargo.

Incandescent – *Glowing*
Chaff – *Teasing, Mocking*
intrude – *Break in*
Melancholy – *Sad*

Rooney has spread his cloak upon the soggy crossing of public opinion, and any Elizabeth who treads upon it is as much a queen as another. Attend to the revelation of the secret. In Rooney's ladies may smoke!

McManus sat down at a vacant table. He paid for the glass of beer that he ordered, tilted his narrow-brimmed derby to the back of his brick-dust head, twined his feet among the rungs of his chair, and heaved a sigh of contentment from the breathing spaces of his innermost soul; for this mud honey was clarified sweetness to his taste. The sham gaiety, the hectic glow of counterfeit hospitality, the self-conscious, joyless laughter, the wine-born warmth, the loud music retrieving the hour from frequent whiles of awful and corroding silence, the presence of well-clothed and frank-eyed beneficiaries of Rooney's removal of the restrictions laid upon the weed, the familiar blended odors of soaked lemon peel, flat beer, and *peau d'Espagne* - all these were manna to Cork McManus, hungry for his week in the desert of the Capulet's high rear room.

A girl, alone, entered Rooney's, glanced around with leisurely swiftness, and sat opposite McManus at his table. Her eyes rested upon him for two seconds in the look with which woman reconnoitres all men whom she for the first time confronts. In that space of time she will decide upon one of two things - either to scream for the police, or that she may marry him later on.

Her brief inspection concluded, the girl laid on the table a worn red morocco shopping bag with the inevitable top-gallant sail of frayed lace handkerchief flying from a corner of it. After she had ordered a small beer from the immediate waiter she took from her bag a box of cigarettes and lighted one with slightly exaggerated ease of manner. Then she looked again in the eyes of Cork McManus and smiled.

Instantly the doom of each was sealed.

The unqualified desire of a man to buy clothes and build fires for a woman for a whole lifetime at first sight of her is not uncommon among that humble portion of humanity that does not care for Bradstreet or coats-of-arms or Shaw's plays. Love at first sight has occurred a time or two in high life; but, as a rule, the extempore mania is to be found among unsophisticated creatures such as the dove, the blue-tailed dingbat, and the ten-dollar-a-week clerk. Poets, subscribers to all fiction magazines, and schatchens, take notice.

Revelation
– *Exposure*
Vacant – *Empty*
Mania – *Obsession*
Unsophisticated –
Simple, Naive

With the exchange of the mysterious magnetic current came to each of them the instant desire to lie, pretend, dazzle and deceive, which is the worst thing about the hypocritical disorder known as love.

"Have another beer?" suggested Cork. In his circle the phrase was considered to be a card, accompanied by a letter of introduction and references.

"No, thanks," said the girl, raising her eyebrows and choosing her conventional words carefully. "I - merely dropped in for - a slight refreshment." The cigarette between her fingers seemed to require explanation. "My aunt is a Russian lady," she concluded, "and we often have a post per annual cigarette after dinner at home."

"Cheese it!" said Cork, whom society airs oppressed. "Your fingers are as yellow as mine."

"Say," said the girl, blazing upon him with low-voiced indignation, "what do you think I am? Say, who do you think you are talking to? What?"

She was pretty to look at. Her eyes were big, brown, intrepid, and bright. Under her flat sailor hat, planted jauntily on one side, her crinkly, tawny hair parted and was drawn back, low and massy, in a thick, pendant knot behind. The roundness of girlhood still lingered in her chin and neck, but her cheeks and fingers were thinning slightly.

She looked upon the world with defiance, suspicion, and sullen wonder. Her smart, short tan coat was soiled and expensive. Two inches below her black dress dropped the lowest flounce of a heliotrope silk underskirt. "Beg your pardon," said Cork, looking at her admiringly. "I didn't mean anything. Sure, it's no harm to smoke, Maudy."

"Rooney's," said the girl, softened at once by his amends, "is the only place I know where a lady can smoke. Maybe it ain't a nice habit, but aunty lets us at home. And my name ain't Maudy, if you please; it's Ruby Delamere."

"That's a swell handle," said Cork approvingly. "Mine's McManus - Cor - er - Eddie McManus."

"Oh, you can't help that," laughed Ruby. "Don't apologize."

Cork looked seriously at the big clock on Rooney's wall. The girl's ubiquitous eyes took in the movement.

Oppress – *Dominate*
Indignation – *Anger*
Defiance – *Disobedience*
Amends – *Improvement*
Ubiquitous – *Omnipresent*

"I know it's late," she said, reaching for her bag; "but you know how you want a smoke when you want one. Ain't Rooney's all right? I never saw anything wrong here. This is twice I've been in. I work in a bookbindery on Third Avenue. A lot of us girls have been working overtime three nights a week. They won't let you smoke there, of course.

I just dropped in here on my way home for a puff. Ain't it all right in here? If it ain't, I won't come any more."

"It's a little bit late for you to be out alone anywhere," said Cork. "I'm not wise to this particular joint; but anyhow you don't want to have your picture taken in it for a present to your Sunday School teacher. Have one more beer, and then say I take you home."

"But I don't know you," said the girl, with fine scrupulosity. "I don't accept the company of gentlemen I ain't acquainted with. My aunt never would allow that."

"Why," said Cork McManus, pulling his ear, "I'm the latest thing in suitings with side vents and bell skirt when it comes to escortin' a lady. You bet you'll find me all right, Ruby. And I'll give you a tip as to who I am. My governor is one of the hottest cross-buns of the Wall Street push. Morgan's cab horse casts a shoe every time the old man sticks his head out the window. Me! Well, I'm in trainin' down the Street.

The old man's goin' to put a seat on the Stock Exchange in my stockin' my next birthday. But it all sounds like a lemon to me. What I like is golf and yachtin' and - er - well, say a corkin' fast ten-round bout between welter-weights with walkin' gloves."

"I guess you can walk to the door with me," said the girl hesitatingly, but with a certain pleased flutter. "Still I never heard anything extra good about Wall Street brokers, or sport who go to prize fights, either. Ain't you got any other recommendations?"

"I think you're the swellest looker I've had my lamps on in little old New York," said Cork impressively. "That'll be about enough of that, now. Ain't you the kidder!" She modified her chiding words by a deep, long, beaming, smile-embellished look at her cavalier. "We'll drink our beer before we go, ha?"

Cavalier – *A horseman, Knight*
Suspended – *Postponed*

A waiter sang. The tobacco smoke grew denser, drifting and rising in spirals, waves, tilted layers, cumulus clouds, cataracts and suspended fogs like some fifth element created from the ribs of the ancient four. Laughter and chat grew louder, stimulated by Rooney's liquids and Rooney's gallant hospitality to Lady Nicotine.

One o'clock struck. Downstairs there was a sound of closing and locking doors. Frank pulled down the green shades of the front windows carefully. Rooney went below in the dark hall and stood at the front door, his cigarette cached in the hollow of his hand. Thenceforth whoever might seek admittance must present a countenance familiar to Rooney's hawk's eye - the countenance of a true sport.

Cork McManus and the bookbindery girl conversed absorbedly, with their elbows on the table. Their glasses of beer were pushed to one side, scarcely touched, with the foam on them sunken to a thin white scum. Since the stroke of one the stale pleasures of Rooney's had become renovated and spiced; not by any addition to the list of distractions, but because from that moment the sweets became stolen ones.

The flattest glass of beer acquired the tang of illegality; the mildest claret punch struck a knockout blow at law and order; the harmless and genial company became outlaws, defying authority and rule. For after the stroke of one in such places as Rooney's, where neither bed nor board is to be had, drink may not be set before the thirsty of the city of the four million. It is the law.

"Say," said Cork McManus, almost covering the table with his eloquent chest and elbows, "was that dead straight about you workin' in the bookbindery and livin' at home - and just happenin' in here - and - and all that spiel you gave me?"

"Sure it was," answered the girl with spirit. "Why, what do you think? Do you suppose I'd lie to you? Go down to the shop and ask 'em. I handed it to you on the level."

"On the dead level?" said Cork. "That's the way I want it; because -"

"Because what?"

"I throw up my hands," said Cork. "You've got me goin'. You're the girl I've been lookin' for. Will you keep company with me, Ruby?"

Countenance –
Tolerate
Acquire – *Obtain*
Defy – *Confront*
Eloquent – *Expressive*

"Would you like me to - Eddie?"

"Surest thing. But I wanted a straight story about - about yourself, you know. When a fellow had a girl - a steady girl - she's got to be all right, you know. She's got to be straight goods."

"You'll find I'll be straight goods, Eddie."

"Of course you will. I believe what you told me. But you can't blame me for wantin' to find out. You don't see many girls smokin' cigarettes in places like Rooney's after midnight that are like you."

The girl flushed a little and lowered her eyes. "I see that now," she said meekly. "I didn't know how bad it looked. But I won't do it anymore. And I'll go straight home every night and stay there. And I'll give up cigarettes if you say so, Eddie - I'll cut 'em out from this minute on."

Cork's air became judicial, proprietary, condemnatory, yet sympathetic. "A lady can smoke," he decided, slowly, "at times and places. Why? Because it's bein' a lady that helps her pull it off."

"I'm going to quit. There's nothing to it," said the girl. She flicked the stub of her cigarette to the floor.

"At times and places," repeated Cork. "When I call round for you of evenin's we'll hunt out a dark bench in Stuyvesant Square and have a puff or two. But no more Rooney's at one o'clock - see?"

"Eddie, do you really like me?" The girl searched his hard but frank features eagerly with anxious eyes.

"On the dead level."

"When are you coming to see me - where I live?"

"Thursday - day after tomorrow evenin'. That suit you?"

"Fine. I'll be ready for you. Come about seven. Walk to the door with me tonight and I'll show you where I live. Don't forget, now. And don't you go to see any other girls before then, mister! I bet you will, though."

"On the dead level," said Cork, "you make 'em all look like rag-dolls to me. Honest, you do. I know when I'm suited. On the dead level, I do."

Against the front door down-stairs repeated heavy blows were delivered. The loud crashes resounded in the room above. Only a trip-hammer or a policeman's foot could have

Meek – *Humble*
Condemnatory –
Disapproving
Anxious – *Nervous*
Assaulted – *A*
sudden, violent attack
Panic – *Fright*

been the author of those sounds. Rooney jumped like a bull-frog to a corner of the room, turned off the electric lights and hurried swiftly below. The room was left utterly dark except for the winking red glow of cigars and cigarettes.

A second volley of crashes came up from the assaulted door. A little, rustling, murmuring panic moved among the besieged guests. Frank, cool, smooth, reassuring, could be seen in the rosy glow of the burning tobacco, going from table to table.

"All keep still!" was his caution. "Don't talk or make any noise! Everything will be allright. Now, don't feel the slightest alarm. We'll take care of you all."

Ruby felt across the table until Cork's firm hand closed upon hers. "Are you afraid, Eddie?" she whispered. "Are you afraid you'll get a free ride?"

"Nothin' doin' in the teeth-chatterin' line," said Cork. "I guess Rooney's been slow with his envelope. Don't you worry, girly; I'll look out for you all right."

Yet Mr. McManus's ease was only skin-and muscle-deep. With the police looking everywhere for Buck Malone's assailant, and with Corrigan still on the ocean wave, he felt that to be caught in a police raid would mean an ended career for him. He wished he had remained in the high rear room of the true Capulet reading the pink extras.

Rooney seemed to have opened the front door below and engaged the police in conference in the dark hall. The wordless low growl of their voices came up the stairway. Frank made a wireless news station of himself at the upper door. Suddenly he closed the door, hurried to the extreme rear of the room and lighted a dim gas jet.

"This way, everybody!" he called sharply. "In a hurry; but no noise, please!"

The guests crowded in confusion to the rear. Rooney's lieutenant swung open a panel in the wall, overlooking the back yard, revealing a ladder already placed for the escape.

"Down and out, everybody!" he commanded. "Ladies first! Less talking, please! Don't crowd! There's no danger."

Among the last, Cork and Ruby waited their turn at the open panel. Suddenly she swept him aside and clung to his arm fiercely.

Assailant – *Attacker*
Fierce – *Violent*
Flee – *Escape*
Descend – *To move/go down*

"Before we go out," she whispered in his ear - "before anything happens, tell me again, Eddie, do you l - do you really like me?"

"On the dead level," said Cork, holding her close with one arm, "when it comes to you, I'm all in."

When they turned they found they were lost and in darkness. The last of the fleeing customers had descended. Half way across the yard they bore the ladder, stumbling, giggling, hurrying to place it against adjoining low building over the roof of which their only route to safety.

"We may as well sit down," said Cork grimly. "Maybe Rooney will stand the cops off, anyhow."

They sat at a table; and their hands came together again.

A number of men then entered the dark room, feeling their way about. One of them, Rooney himself, found the switch and turned on the electric light. The other man was a cop of the old regime - a big cop, a thick cop, a fuming, abrupt cop - not a pretty cop. He went up to the pair at the table and sneered familiarly at the girl.

"What are you doin' in here?" he asked.

"Dropped in for a smoke," said Cork mildly.

"Had any drinks?"

"Not later than one o'clock."

"Get out - quick!" ordered the cop. Then, "Sit down!" he countermanded.

He took off Cork's hat roughly and scrutinized him shrewdly. "Your name's McManus."

"Bad guess," said Cork. "It's Peterson."

"Cork McManus, or something like that," said the cop. "You put a knife into a man in Dutch Mike's saloon a week ago."

"Aw, forget it!" said Cork, who perceived a shade of doubt in the officer's tones. "You've got my mug mixed with somebody else's."

"Have I? Well, you'll come to the station with me, anyhow, and be looked over. The description fits you all right." The cop twisted his fingers under Cork's collar. "Come on!" he ordered roughly.

Cork glanced at Ruby. She was pale, and her thin nostrils quivered. Her quick eye danced from one man's face

Abrupt – *Sudden*
Countermanded – *Cancelled*
Shrewdly – *Astutely*
Stumble – *To trip or fall while walking/ running*
Fury – *Anger*

Greatest   Love   Stories

to the other as they spoke or moved. What hard luck! Cork was thinking - Corrigan on the briny; and Ruby met and lost almost within an hour! Somebody at the police station would recognize him, without a doubt. Hard luck!

But suddenly the girl sprang up and hurled herself with both arms extended against the cop. His hold on Cork's collar was loosened and he stumbled back two or three paces.

"Don't go so fast, Maguire!" she cried in shrill fury. "Keep your hands off my man! You know me, and you know I'm givin' you good advice. Don't you touch him again! He's not the guy you are lookin' for - I'll stand for that."

"See here, Fanny," said the Cop, red and angry, "I'll take you, too, if you don't look out! How do you know this ain't the man I want? What are you doing in here with him?"

"How do I know?" said the girl, flaming red and white by turns. "Because I've known him a year. He's mine. Oughtn't I to know? And what am I doin' here with him? That's easy."

She stooped low and reached down somewhere into a swirl of flirted draperies, heliotrope and black. An elastic snapped, she threw on the table toward Cork a folded wad of bills. The money slowly straightened itself with little leisurely jerks.

"Take that, Jimmy, and let's go," said the girl. "I'm declarin' the usual dividends, Maguire," she said to the officer. "You had your usual five-dollar graft at the usual corner at ten."

"A lie!" said the cop, turning purple. "You go on my beat again and I'll arrest you every time I see you."

"No, you won't," said the girl. "And I'll tell you why. Witnesses saw me give you the money tonight, and last week, too. I've been getting fixed for you."

Cork put the wad of money carefully into his pocket, and said, "Come on, Fanny; let's have some chop suey before we go home."

"Clear out, quick, both of you, or I'll -"

The cop's bluster trailed away into inconsequentiality.

At the corner of the street the two halted. Cork handed back the money without a word. The girl took it and slipped it slowly into her hand bag.

Her expression was the same she had worn when she entered Rooney's that night - she looked upon the world with defiance, suspicion, and sullen wonder.

Leisurely – *Unhurried*
Halt – *Stop*
Defiance –
Disobedience
Sullen – *Gloomy*

"I guess I might as well say good-bye here," she said dully. "You won't want to see me again, of course. Will you - shake hands - Mr. McManus."

"I mightn't have got wise if you hadn't give the snap away," said Cork. "Why did you do it?"

"You'd have been pinched if I hadn't. That's why. Ain't that reason enough?" Then she began to cry. "Honest, Eddie, I was goin' to be the best girl in the world.

I hated to be what I am; I hated men; I was ready almost to die when I saw you. And you seemed different from everybody else. And when I found you liked me, too, why, I thought I'd make you believe I was good, and I was goin' to be good.

When you asked to come to my house and see me, why, I'd have died rather than do anything wrong after that. But what's the use of talking about it? I'll say good-bye, if you will, Mr. McManus."

Cork was pulling at his ear. "I knifed Malone," said he. "I was the one the cop wanted."

"Oh, that's all right," said the girl listlessly. "It didn't make any difference about that."

"That was all hot air about Wall Street. I don't do nothin' but hang out with a tough gang on the East Side."

"That was all right, too," repeated the girl. "It didn't make any difference."

Cork straightened himself, and pulled his hat down low. "I could get a job at O'Brien's," he said aloud, but to himself.

"Good-bye," said the girl.

"Come on," said Cork, taking her arm. "I know a place."

Two blocks away he turned with her up the steps of a red brick house facing a little park. "What house is this?" she asked, drawing back. "Why are you going in there?"

A street lamp shone brightly in front. There was a brass nameplate at one side of the closed front doors. Cork drew her firmly up the steps. "Read that," said he.

She looked at the name on the plate, and gave a cry between a moan and a scream. "No, no, no, Eddie! Oh, my God, no! I won't let you do that - not now! Let me go! You shan't

Listless – *Languid*
Moan – *Groan*
Gruffly – *Grumpily*
cunning – *Sly*

do that! You can't - you mus'n't! Not after you know! No, no! Come away quick! Oh, my God! Please, Eddie, come!"

Half fainting, she reeled, and was caught in the bend of his arm. Cork's right hand felt for the electric button and pressed it long.

Another cop - how quickly they scent trouble when trouble is on the wing! - came along, saw them, and ran up the steps. "Here! What are you doing with that girl?" he called gruffly.

"She'll be all right in a minute," said Cork. "It's a straight deal."

"Reverend Jeremiah Jones," read the cop from the door-plate with true detective cunning.

"Correct," said Cork. "On the dead level, we're goin' to get married."

Detective – *A person* *crime*
Cop– *Police*
Reeled – *To have a* *sensation of whirling*

Food For Thought

"I am going to quit. There's nothing to it." Who said this? What did she want to quit? Do you think that Ruby Delamere was actually a book-bindery girl? Had she fallen dep in love with Eddie McManus?

An Understanding

Q. 1. Who was Eddie McManus? What was he popularly known as? What did he do and why were the cops looking for him?

Ans. _____

_____

_____

_____

_____

Q. 2. What was the real identity of Eddie McManus or Cork McManus? Who was Ruby Delamere?

Ans. _____

_____

_____

_____

_____

Q. 3. What sort of a girl was Ruby Delamere? Why did she faint when she looked at the name on the nameplate of the house to which Cork drew her up the steps?

Ans. _____

_____

_____

_____

_____

Q. 4. Why did the author, O. Henry keep the name of the story as "Past One At Rodneys?' Who was Rodney and how was the place where Eddie McManus and the girl, Ruby Delamere met? What happened at one o'clock

Ans. _____

_____

_____

_____

_____

Nathaniel Hawthorne

Born on July 4, 1804
Died on May 19, 1864
Notable Works: *Twice-Told Tales, Grandfather's Chair, Mosses from an Old Manse, etc.* are some of his famous short stories. *The Scarlet Letter, The House of the Seven Gables, The Blithedale Romance* and *The Marble Faun* are some of his popular novels.

Early Life

Nathaniel Hawthorne was a great American novelist and short story writer. He was born on July 4, 1804, in Salem, Massachusetts in the city of Salem, Massachusetts. His ancestors include John Hathorne, the only judge involved in the Salem witch trials who never repented of his actions. Nathaniel later added a "w" to make his name, "Hawthorne" in order to hide this relation. He entered Bowdoin College in 1821, was elected to Phi Beta Kappa in 1824, and graduated in 1825.

Literary Works and Achievements

Hawthorne anonymously published his first work, a novel titled *Fanshawe*, in 1828. He published several short stories in various periodicals which he collected in 1837 as *Twice-Told Tales. Grandfather's Chair, Mosses from an Old Manse, etc.* are some of his famous short stories. n 1836 Hawthorne served as the editor of the *American Magazine of Useful and Entertaining Knowledge.*

The Scarlet Letter was published in 1850, followed by a succession of other novels. Some of his other popular works are: *The House of the Seven Gables* (1851), *The Blithedale Romance* (1852) and *The Marble Faun* (1860), and many more.

Writing Style

Much of Hawthorne's writing centers on New England, many works featuring moral allegories with a Puritan inspiration. His fiction works are considered part of the Romantic Movement and, more specifically, dark romanticism. His themes often centre on the inherent evil and sin of humanity, and his works often have moral messages and deep psychological complexity. His published works include novels, short stories, and a biography of his friend.

Later Years

A political appointment took Hawthorne and family to Europe before their return to The Wayside in 1860. Hawthorne died on May 19, 1864, and was survived by his wife and their three children. Longfellow wrote a tribute poem to Hawthorne, published in 1866, called *The Bells of Lynn*. Hawthorne was buried on what is now known as "Authors' Ridge" in Sleepy Hollow Cemetery, Concord, Massachusetts.

Trivia

Hawthorne also wrote non-fiction. In 2008, The Library of America selected Hawthorne's "A Collection of Wax Figures" for inclusion in its two-century retrospective of American True Crime.

Rappaccini's Daughter

~Nathaniel Hawthorne

WE do not remember to have seen any translated speci- mens of the productions of M. de l'Aubepine -- a fact the less to be wondered at, as his very name is unknown to many of his own countrymen as well as to the student of foreign literature. As a writer, he seems to occupy an unfor- tunate position between the Transcendentalists (who, under one name or another, have their share in all the current litera- ture of the world) and the great body of pen-and-ink men who address the intellect and sympathies of the multitude. If not too refined, at all events too remote, too shadowy, and unsubstantial in his modes of development to suit the taste of the latter class, and yet too popular to satisfy the spiritual or metaphysical requisitions of the former, he must necessarily find himself without an audience, except here and there an individual or possibly an isolated clique. His writings, to do them justice, are not altogether destitute of fancy and origi- nality; they might have won him greater reputation but for an inveterate love of allegory, which is apt to invest his plots and characters with the aspect of scenery and people in the clouds, and to steal away the human warmth out of his con- ceptions. His fictions are sometimes historical, sometimes of the present day, and sometimes, so far as can be discovered, have little or no reference either to time or space. In any case, he generally contents himself with a very slight embroidery of outward manners, -- the faintest possible counterfeit of real life, -- and endeavors to create an interest by some less obvi- ous peculiarity of the subject. Occasionally a breath of Nature, a raindrop of pathos and tenderness, or a gleam of humor, will find its way into the midst of his fantastic imagery, and make us feel as if, after all, we were yet within the limits of our native earth. We will only add to this very cursory notice that M. de l'Aubepine's productions, if the reader chance to take them in precisely the proper point of view, may amuse a leisure hour as well as those of a brighter man; if otherwise, they can hardly fail to look excessively like nonsense.

Our author is voluminous; he continues to write and pub- lish with as much praiseworthy and indefatigable prolixity as

Specimen – *Example*
Unfortunate –
Unlucky
Intellect
– *Intelligence*
Isolate – *Separate*
Indefatigable –
Untiring,
inexhaustible

if his efforts were crowned with the brilliant success that so justly attends those of Eugene Sue. His first appearance was by a collection of stories in a long series of volumes entitled "Contes deux fois racontees." The titles of some of his more recent works (we quote from memory) are as follows: "Le Voyage Celeste a Chemin de Fer," 3 tom., 1838; "Le nouveau Pere Adam et la nouvelle Mere Eve," 2 tom., 1839; "Roderic; ou le Serpent a l'estomac," 2 tom., 1840; "Le Culte du Feu," a folio volume of ponderous research into the religion and ritual of the old Persian Ghebers, published in 1841; "La Soiree du Chateau en Espagne," 1 tom., 8vo, 1842; and "L'Artiste du Beau; ou le Papillon Mecanique," 5 tom., 4to, 1843. Our somewhat wearisome perusal of this startling catalogue of volumes has left behind it a certain personal affection and sympathy, though by no means admiration, for M. de l'Aubepine; and we would fain do the little in our power towards introducing him favorably to the American public. The ensuing tale is a translation of his "Beatrice; ou la Belle Empoisonneuse," recently published in "La Revue Anti-Aristocratique." This journal, edited by the Comte de Bearhaven, has for some years past led the defence of liberal principles and popular rights with a faithfulness and ability worthy of all praise.

A young man, named Giovanni Guasconti, came, very long ago, from the more southern region of Italy, to pursue his studies at the University of Padua. Giovanni, who had but a scanty supply of gold ducats in his pocket, took lodgings in a high and gloomy chamber of an old edifice which looked not unworthy to have been the palace of a Paduan noble, and which, in fact, exhibited over its entrance the armorial bearings of a family long since extinct. The young stranger, who was not unstudied in the great poem of his country, recollected that one of the ancestors of this family, and perhaps an occupant of this very mansion, had been pictured by Dante as a partaker of the immortal agonies of his Inferno. These reminiscences and associations, together with the tendency to heartbreak natural to a young man for the first time out of his native sphere, caused Giovanni to sigh heavily as he looked around the desolate and ill-furnished apartment.

"Holy Virgin, signor!" cried old Dame Lisabetta, who, won by the youth's remarkable beauty of person, was kindly endeavoring to give the chamber a habitable air, "what a sigh was that to come out of a young man's heart! Do you find

Wearisome
– *Tiresome*
Perusal
– *Examination*
Desolate – *Isolated*

this old mansion gloomy? For the love of Heaven, then, put your head out of the window, and you will see as bright sunshine as you have left in Naples."

Guasconti mechanically did as the old woman advised, but could not quite agree with her that the Paduan sunshine was as cheerful as that of southern Italy. Such as it was, however, it fell upon a garden beneath the window and expended its fostering influences on a variety of plants, which seemed to have been cultivated with exceeding care.

"Does this garden belong to the house?" asked Giovanni.

"Heaven forbid, signor, unless it were fruitful of better pot herbs than any that grow there now," answered old Lisabetta. "No; that garden is cultivated by the own hands of Signor Giacomo Rappaccini, the famous doctor, who, I warrant him, has been heard of as far as Naples. It is said that he distils these plants into medicines that are as potent as a charm. Oftentimes you may see the signor doctor at work, and perchance the signora, his daughter, too, gathering the strange flowers that grow in the garden."

The old woman had now done what she could for the aspect of the chamber; and, commending the young man to the protection of the saints, took her departure.

Giovanni still found no better occupation than to look down into the garden beneath his window. From its appearance, he judged it to be one of those botanic gardens which were of earlier date in Padua than elsewhere in Italy or in the world. Or, not improbably, it might once have been the pleasure-place of an opulent family; for there was the ruin of a marble fountain in the centre, sculptured with rare art, but so woefully shattered that it was impossible to trace the original design from the chaos of remaining fragments. The water, however, continued to gush and sparkle into the sunbeams as cheerfully as ever. A little gurgling sound ascended to the young man's window, and made him feel as if the fountain were an immortal spirit that sung its song unceasingly and without heeding the vicissitudes around it, while one century imbodied it in marble and another scattered the perishable garniture on the soil. All about the pool into which the water subsided grew various plants, that seemed to require a plentiful supply of moisture for the nourishment of gigantic leaves, and in some instances, flowers gorgeously magnificent. There was one shrub in particular, set in a marble vase in the midst of the pool, that bore a profusion of purple blossoms, each

commend – *Praise*
Opulent – *Wealthy*
Chaos – *Confusion*
Unceasing – *Interminable*
Perishable – *Liable to rot/wither*

of which had the luster and richness of a gem; and the whole together made a show so resplendent that it seemed enough to illuminate the garden, even had there been no sunshine. Every portion of the soil was peopled with plants and herbs, which, if less beautiful, still bore tokens of assiduous care, as if all had their individual virtues, known to the scientific mind that fostered them. Some were placed in urns, rich with old carving, and others in common garden pots; some crept serpent-like along the ground or climbed on high, using whatever means of ascent was offered them. One plant had wreathed itself round a statue of Vertumnus, which was thus quite veiled and shrouded in a drapery of hanging foliage, so happily arranged that it might have served a sculptor for a study.

While Giovanni stood at the window he heard a rustling behind a screen of leaves, and became aware that a person was at work in the garden. His figure soon emerged into view, and showed itself to be that of no common laborer, but a tall, emaciated, sallow, and sickly-looking man, dressed in a scholar's garb of black. He was beyond the middle term of life, with gray hair, a thin, gray beard, and a face singularly marked with intellect and cultivation, but which could never, even in his more youthful days, have expressed much warmth of heart.

Nothing could exceed the intentness with which this scientific gardener examined every shrub which grew in his path. It seemed as if he was looking into their inmost nature, making observations in regard to their creative essence, and discovering why one leaf grew in this shape and another in that, and wherefore such and such flowers differed among themselves in hue and perfume. Nevertheless, in spite of this deep intelligence on his part, there was no approach to intimacy between himself and these vegetable existences. On the contrary, he avoided their actual touch or the direct inhaling of their odors with a caution that impressed Giovanni most disagreeably; for the man's demeanor was that of one walking among malignant influences, such as savage beasts, or deadly snakes, or evil spirits, which, should he allow them one moment of license, would wreak upon him some terrible fatality. It was strangely frightful to the young man's imagination to see this air of insecurity in a person cultivating a garden, that most simple and innocent of human toils, and which had been alike the joy and labor of the unfallen parents of the race. Was this garden, then, the Eden of the present world? And

Profusion – *Abundance*
Luster – *Sheen*
Intentness – *Attentiveness*
Inmost – *Innermost*
Demeanour *– Behaviour*

this man, with such a perception of harm in what his own hands caused to grow, -- was he the Adam?

The distrustful gardener, while plucking away the dead leaves or pruning the too luxuriant growth of the shrubs, defended his hands with a pair of thick gloves. Nor were these his only armor. When, in his walk through the garden, he came to the magnificent plant that hung its purple gems beside the marble fountain, he placed a kind of mask over his mouth and nostrils, as if all this beauty did but conceal a deadlier malice; but, finding his task still too dangerous, he drew back, removed the mask, and called loudly, but in the infirm voice of a person affected with inward disease, "Beatrice! Beatrice!"

"Here am I, my father. What would you?" cried a rich and youthful voice from the window of the opposite house -- a voice as rich as a tropical sunset, and which made Giovanni, though he knew not why, think of deep hues of purple or crimson and of perfumes heavily delectable. "Are you in the garden?"

"Yes, Beatrice," answered the gardener, "and I need your help."

Soon there emerged from under a sculptured portal the figure of a young girl, arrayed with as much richness of taste as the most splendid of the flowers, beautiful as the day, and with a bloom so deep and vivid that one shade more would have been too much. She looked redundant with life, health, and energy; all of which attributes were bound down and compressed, as it were and girdled tensely, in their luxuriance, by her virgin zone. Yet Giovanni's fancy must have grown morbid while he looked down into the garden; for the impression which the fair stranger made upon him was as if here were another flower, the human sister of those vegetable ones, as beautiful as they, more beautiful than the richest of them, but still to be touched only with a glove, nor to be approached without a mask. As Beatrice came down the garden path, it was observable that she handled and inhaled the odor of several of the plants which her father had most sedulously avoided.

"Here, Beatrice," said the latter, "see how many needful offices require to be done to our chief treasure. Yet, shattered as I am, my life might pay the penalty of approaching it so closely as circumstances demand. Henceforth, I fear, this plant must be consigned to your sole charge."

Conceal – *Hide*
Malice – *Hatred*
Delectable – *Delicious*
Redundant – *Old and useless*
Morbid – *Diseased, Unhealthy*

"And gladly will I undertake it," cried again the rich tones of the young lady, as she bent towards the magnificent plant and opened her arms as if to embrace it. "Yes, my sister, my splendour, it shall be Beatrice's task to nurse and serve thee; and thou shalt reward her with thy kisses and perfumed breath, which to her is as the breath of life."

Then, with all the tenderness in her manner that was so strikingly expressed in her words, she busied herself with such attentions as the plant seemed to require; and Giovanni, at his lofty window, rubbed his eyes and almost doubted whether it were a girl tending her favorite flower, or one sister performing the duties of affection to another. The scene soon terminated. Whether Dr. Rappaccini had finished his labors in the garden, or that his watchful eye had caught the stranger's face, he now took his daughter's arm and retired. Night was already closing in; oppressive exhalations seemed to proceed from the plants and steal upward past the open window; and Giovanni, closing the lattice, went to his couch and dreamed of a rich flower and beautiful girl. Flower and maiden were different, and yet the same, and fraught with some strange peril in either shape.

But there is an influence in the light of morning that tends to rectify whatever errors of fancy, or even of judgment, we may have incurred during the sun's decline, or among the shadows of the night, or in the less wholesome glow of moonshine. Giovanni's first movement, on starting from sleep, was to throw open the window and gaze down into the garden which his dreams had made so fertile of mysteries. He was surprised and a little ashamed to find how real and matter-of-fact an affair it proved to be, in the first rays of the sun which gilded the dew drops that hung upon leaf and blossom, and, while giving a brighter beauty to each rare flower, brought everything within the limits of ordinary experience. The young man rejoiced that, in the heart of the barren city, he had the privilege of overlooking this spot of lovely and luxuriant vegetation. It would serve, he said to himself, as a symbolic language to keep him in communion with Nature. Neither the sickly and thoughtworn Dr. Giacomo Rappaccini, it is true, nor his brilliant daughter, were now visible; so that Giovanni could not determine how much of the singularity which he attributed to both was due to their own qualities and how much to his wonder-working fancy; but he was inclined to take a most rational view of the whole matter.

Consign – *Commit*
Terminate – *To agree*
Peril – *Risk*
Rectify – *Cure*
Rejoice – *Exult, Glory*

In the course of the day he paid his respects to Signor Pietro Baglioni, professor of medicine in the university, a physician of eminent repute to whom Giovanni had brought a letter of introduction. The professor was an elderly personage, apparently of genial nature, and habits that might almost be called jovial. He kept the young man to dinner, and made himself very agreeable by the freedom and liveliness of his conversation, especially when warmed by a flask or two of Tuscan wine. Giovanni, conceiving that men of science, inhabitants of the same city, must be on familiar terms with one another, took an opportunity to mention the name of Dr. Rappaccini. But the professor did not respond with so much cordiality as he had anticipated.

"Ill would it become a teacher of the divine art of medicine," said Professor Pietro Baglioni, in answer to a question of Giovanni, "to withhold due and well-considered praise of a physician so eminently skilled as Rappaccini; but, on the other hand, I should answer it but scantily to my conscience were I to permit a worthy youth like yourself, Signor Giovanni, the son of an ancient friend, to imbibe erroneous ideas respecting a man who might hereafter chance to hold your life and death in his hands. The truth is, our worshipful Dr. Rappaccini has as much science as any member of the faculty -- with perhaps one single exception -- in Padua, or all Italy; but there are certain grave objections to his professional character."

"And what are they?" asked the young man.

"Has my friend Giovanni any disease of body or heart, that he is so inquisitive about physicians?" said the professor, with a smile. "But as for Rappaccini, it is said of him -- and I, who know the man well, can answer for its truth -- that he cares infinitely more for science than for mankind. His patients are interesting to him only as subjects for some new experiment. He would sacrifice human life, his own among the rest, or whatever else was dearest to him, for the sake of adding so much as a grain of mustard seed to the great heap of his accumulated knowledge."

"Me thinks he is an awful man indeed," remarked Guasconti, mentally recalling the cold and purely intellectual aspect of Rappaccini. "And yet, worshipful professor, is it not a noble spirit? Are there many men capable of so spiritual a love of science?"

"God forbid," answered the professor, somewhat testily; "at least, unless they take sounder views of the healing art than those

Conceiving –
Forming
Cordiality
– *Friendliness*
Anticipate
– *Antedate*
Imbibe – *Swallow*
Accumulate – *Accrue*

adopted by Rappaccini. It is his theory that all medicinal virtues are comprised within those substances which we term vegetable poisons. These he cultivates with his own hands, and is said even to have produced new varieties of poison, more horribly deleterious than Nature, without the assistance of this learned person, would ever have plagued the world withal. That the signor doctor does less mischief than might be expected with such dangerous substances is undeniable. Now and then, it must be owned, he has effected, or seemed to effect, a marvellous cure; but, to tell you my private mind, Signor Giovanni, he should receive little credit for such instances of success, -- they being probably the work of chance, -- but should be held strictly accountable for his failures, which may justly be considered his own work."

The youth might have taken Baglioni's opinions with many grains of allowance had he known that there was a professional warfare of long continuance between him and Dr. Rappaccini, in which the latter was generally thought to have gained the advantage. If the reader be inclined to judge for himself, we refer him to certain black-letter tracts on both sides, preserved in the medical department of the University of Padua.

"I know not, most learned professor," returned Giovanni, after musing on what had been said of Rappaccini's exclusive zeal for science, --"I know not how dearly this physician may love his art; but surely there is one object more dear to him. He has a daughter."

"Aha!" cried the professor, with a laugh. "So now our friend Giovanni's secret is out. You have heard of this daughter, whom all the young men in Padua are wild about, though not half a dozen have ever had the good hap to see her face. I know little of the Signora Beatrice save that Rappaccini is said to have instructed her deeply in his science, and that, young and beautiful as fame reports her, she is already qualified to fill a professor's chair. Perchance her father destines her for mine! Other absurd rumors there be, not worth talking about or listening to. So now, Signor Giovanni, drink off your glass of lachryma."

Guasconti returned to his lodgings somewhat heated with the wine he had quaffed, and which caused his brain to swim with strange fantasies in reference to Dr. Rappaccini and the beautiful Beatrice. On his way, happening to pass by a florist's, he bought a fresh bouquet of flowers.

Deleterious – *Harmful*
plagued – *Overwhelmed*
Credit – *Praise*
Youth – *Childhood*
Incline – *Slope*

Ascending to his chamber, he seated himself near the window, but within the shadow thrown by the depth of the wall, so that he could look down into the garden with little risk of being discovered. All beneath his eye was a solitude. The strange plants were basking in the sunshine, and now and then nodding gently to one another, as if in acknowledgment of sympathy and kindred. In the midst, by the shattered fountain, grew the magnificent shrub, with its purple gems clustering all over it; they glowed in the air, and gleamed back again out of the depths of the pool, which thus seemed to overflow with colored radiance from the rich reflection that was steeped in it. At first, as we have said, the garden was a solitude. Soon, however, -- as Giovanni had half hoped, half feared, would be the case, -- a figure appeared beneath the antique sculptured portal, and came down between the rows of plants, inhaling their various perfumes as if she were one of those beings of old classic fable that lived upon sweet odors. On again beholding Beatrice, the young man was even startled to perceive how much her beauty exceeded his recollection of it; so brilliant, so vivid, was its character, that she glowed amid the sunlight, and, as Giovanni whispered to himself, positively illuminated the more shadowy intervals of the garden path. Her face being now more revealed than on the former occasion, he was struck by its expression of simplicity and sweetness, -- qualities that had not entered into his idea of her character, and which made him ask anew what manner of mortal she might be. Nor did he fail again to observe, or imagine, an analogy between the beautiful girl and the gorgeous shrub that hung its gem-like flowers over the fountain, -- a resemblance which Beatrice seemed to have indulged a fantastic humor in heightening, both by the arrangement of her dress and the selection of its hues.

Approaching the shrub, she threw open her arms, as with a passionate ardour, and drew its branches into an intimate embrace -- so intimate that her features were hidden in its leafy bosom and her glistening ringlets all intermingled with the flowers.

"Give me thy breath, my sister," exclaimed Beatrice; "for I am faint with common air. And give me this flower of thine, which I separate with gentlest fingers from the stem and place it close beside my heart."

With these words the beautiful daughter of Rappaccini plucked one of the richest blossoms of the shrub, and was about

Solitude – *Loneliness*
Magnificent – *Wonderful*
Gleam – *Shine*
Perceive – *Notice*
Vivid – *Rich*

to fasten it in her bosom. But now, unless Giovanni's draughts of wine had bewildered his senses, a singular incident occurred. A small orange-colored reptile, of the lizard or chameleon species, chanced to be creeping along the path, just at the feet of Beatrice. It appeared to Giovanni, -- but, at the distance from which he gazed, he could scarcely have seen anything so minute, -- it appeared to him, however, that a drop or two of moisture from the broken stem of the flower descended upon the lizard's head. For an instant the reptile contorted itself violently, and then lay motionless in the sunshine. Beatrice observed this remarkable phenomenon and crossed herself, sadly, but without surprise; nor did she therefore hesitate to arrange the fatal flower in her bosom. There it blushed, and almost glimmered with the dazzling effect of a precious stone, adding to her dress and aspect the one appropriate charm which nothing else in the world could have supplied. But Giovanni, out of the shadow of his window, bent forward and shrank back, and murmured and trembled.

"Am I awake? Have I my senses?" said he to himself. "What is this being? Beautiful shall I call her, or inexpressibly terrible?"

Beatrice now strayed carelessly through the garden, approaching closer beneath Giovanni's window, so that he was compelled to thrust his head quite out of its concealment in order to gratify the intense and painful curiosity which she excited. At this moment there came a beautiful insect over the garden wall; it had, perhaps, wandered through the city, and found no flowers or verdure among those antique haunts of men until the heavy perfumes of Dr. Rappaccini's shrubs had lured it from afar. Without alighting on the flowers, this winged brightness seemed to be attracted by Beatrice, and lingered in the air and fluttered about her head. Now, here it could not be but that Giovanni Guasconti's eyes deceived him. Be that as it might, he fancied that, while Beatrice was gazing at the insect with childish delight, it grew faint and fell at her feet; its bright wings shivered; it was dead -- from no cause that he could discern, unless it were the atmosphere of her breath. Again Beatrice crossed herself and sighed heavily as she bent over the dead insect.

An impulsive movement of Giovanni drew her eyes to the window. There she beheld the beautiful head of the young man -- rather a Grecian than an Italian head, with fair, regular features, and a glistening of gold among his ringlets -- gazing down upon her like a being that hovered in mid air. Scarcely knowing what

Ardour – *Passion*
Bewildered – *Confused*
Contorted – *Knotted*
Verdure – *Greenery*
Alighting – *Landing*

he did, Giovanni threw down the bouquet which he had hitherto held in his hand.

"Signora," said he, "there are pure and healthful flowers. Wear them for the sake of Giovanni Guasconti." "Thanks, signor," replied Beatrice, with her rich voice, that came forth as it were like a gush of music, and with a mirthful expression half childish and half woman-like. "I accept your gift, and would fain recompense it with this precious purple flower; but if I toss it into the air it will not reach you. So Signor Guasconti must even content himself with my thanks."

She lifted the bouquet from the ground, and then, as if inwardly ashamed at having stepped aside from her maidenly reserve to respond to a stranger's greeting, passed swiftly homeward through the garden. But few as the moments were, it seemed to Giovanni, when she was on the point of vanishing beneath the sculptured portal, that his beautiful bouquet was already beginning to wither in her grasp. It was an idle thought; there could be no possibility of distinguishing a faded flower from a fresh one at so great a distance.

For many days after this incident the young man avoided the window that looked into Dr. Rappaccini's garden, as if something ugly and monstrous would have blasted his eyesight had he been betrayed into a glance. He felt conscious of having put himself, to a certain extent, within the influence of an unintelligible power by the communication which he had opened with Beatrice. The wisest course would have been, if his heart were in any real danger, to quit his lodgings and Padua itself at once; the next wiser, to have accustomed himself, as far as possible, to the familiar and daylight view of Beatrice -- thus bringing her rigidly and systematically within the limits of ordinary experience. Least of all, while avoiding her sight, ought Giovanni to have remained so near this extraordinary being that the proximity and possibility even of intercourse should give a kind of substance and reality to the wild vagaries which his imagination ran riot continually in producing. Guasconti had not a deep heart -- or, at all events, its depths were not sounded now; but he had a quick fancy, and an ardent southern temperament, which rose every instant to a higher fever pitch. Whether or no Beatrice possessed those terrible attributes, that fatal breath, the affinity with those so beautiful and deadly flowers which were indicated by what Giovanni had witnessed, she had at least instilled a fierce and subtle poison into his system. It was not love, although her

Deceive – *To mislead, Dupe*
Discern – *To recognise/perceive*
Impulsive – *Rash, Hasty*
Recompense – *To repay payment*
Betray – *To be unfaithful*

rich beauty was a madness to him; nor horror, even while he fancied her spirit to be imbued with the same baneful essence that seemed to pervade her physical frame; but a wild offspring of both love and horror that had each parent in it, and burned like one and shivered like the other. Giovanni knew not what to dread; still less did he know what to hope; yet hope and dread kept a continual warfare in his breast, alternately vanquishing one another and starting up afresh to renew the contest. Blessed are all simple emotions, be they dark or bright! It is the lurid intermixture of the two that produces the illuminating blaze of the infernal regions.

Sometimes he endeavored to assuage the fever of his spirit by a rapid walk through the streets of Padua or beyond its gates. His footsteps kept time with the throbbing of his brain, so that the walk was apt to accelerate itself to a race. One day he found himself arrested; his arm was seized by a portly personage, who had turned back on recognizing the young man and expended much breath in overtaking him.

"Signor Giovanni! Stay, my young friend!" cried he. "Have you forgotten me? That might well be the case if I were as much altered as yourself."

It was Baglioni, whom Giovanni had avoided ever since their first meeting, from a doubt that the professor's sagacity would look too deeply into his secrets. Endeavoring to recover himself, he stared forth wildly from his inner world into the outer one and spoke like a man in a dream.

"Yes; I am Giovanni Guasconti. You are Professor Pietro Baglioni. Now let me pass!"

"Not yet, not yet, Signor Giovanni Guasconti," said the professor, smiling, but at the same time scrutinizing the youth with an earnest glance. "What! Did I grow up side by side with your father? And shall his son pass me like a stranger in these old streets of Padua? Stand still, Signor Giovanni; for we must have a word or two before we part."

"Speedily, then, most worshipful professor, speedily," said Giovanni, with feverish impatience. "Does not your worship see that I am in haste?"

Now, while he was speaking there came a man in black along the street, stooping and moving feebly like a person in inferior health. His face was all overspread with a most sickly and sallow hue, but yet so pervaded with an expression of piercing

Ardent – *Passionate*
Pervade – *Permeate*
Vanquish – *Conquer*
Assuage – *To appease, Satisfy*

and active intellect that an observer might easily have over-looked the merely physical attributes and have seen only this wonderful energy. As he passed, this person exchanged a cold and distant salutation with Baglioni, but fixed his eyes upon Giovanni with an intentness that seemed to bring out whatever was within him worthy of notice. Nevertheless, there was a peculiar quietness in the look, as if taking merely a speculative, not a human interest, in the young man.

"It is Dr. Rappaccini!" whispered the professor when the stranger had passed. "Has he ever seen your face before?"

"Not that I know," answered Giovanni, starting at the name.

"He *has* seen you! he must have seen you!" said Baglioni, hastily. "For some purpose or other, this man of science is making a study of you. I know that look of his! It is the same that coldly illuminates his face as he bends over a bird, a mouse, or a butterfly, which, in pursuance of some experiment, he has killed by the perfume of a flower; a look as deep as Nature itself, but without Nature's warmth of love. Signor Giovanni, I will stake my life upon it, you are the subject of one of Rappaccini's experiments!"

"Will you make a fool of me?" cried Giovanni, passionately. "that, signor professor, were an untoward experiment."

"Patience! Patience!" replied the imperturbable professor. "I tell thee, my poor Giovanni, that Rappaccini has a scientific interest in thee. Thou hast fallen into fearful hands! And the Signora Beatrice, -- what part does she act in this mystery?"

But Guasconti, finding Baglioni's pertinacity intolerable, here broke away, and was gone before the professor could again seize his arm. He looked after the young man intently and shook his head.

"This must not be," said Baglioni to himself. "The youth is the son of my old friend, and shall not come to any harm from which the arcana of medical science can preserve him. Besides, it is too insufferable an impertinence in Rappaccini, thus to snatch the lad out of my own hands, as I may say, and make use of him for his infernal experiments. This daughter of his! It shall be looked to. Perchance, most learned Rappaccini, I may foil you where you little dream of it!"

Meanwhile Giovanni had pursued a circuitous route, and at length found himself at the door of his lodgings. As he crossed the threshold he was met by old Lisabetta, who smirked and smiled, and was evidently desirous to attract his attention;

Earnest – *Solemn*
Feeble – *Weak*
Pervade – *Permeate*
Peculiar – *Odd*
Pursuance –
Enactment, The carrying out of some plan

vainly, however, as the ebullition of his feelings had momentarily subsided into a cold and dull vacuity. He turned his eyes full upon the withered face that was puckering itself into a smile, but seemed to behold it not. The old dame, therefore, laid her grasp upon his cloak.

"Signor! Signor!" whispered she, still with a smile over the whole breadth of her visage, so that it looked not unlike a grotesque carving in wood, darkened by centuries. "Listen, signor! There is a private entrance into the garden!"

"What do you say?" exclaimed Giovanni, turning quickly about, as if an inanimate thing should start into feverish life. "A private entrance into Dr. Rappaccini's garden?"

"Hush! Hush! Not so loud!" whispered Lisabetta, putting her hand over his mouth. "Yes; into the worshipful doctor's garden, where you may see all his fine shrubbery. Many a young man in Padua would give gold to be admitted among those flowers."

Giovanni put a piece of gold into her hand.

"Show me the way," said he.

A surmise, probably excited by his conversation with Baglioni, crossed his mind, that this interposition of old Lisabetta might perchance be connected with the intrigue, whatever were its nature, in which the professor seemed to suppose that Dr. Rappaccini was involving him. But such a suspicion, though it disturbed Giovanni, was inadequate to restrain him. The instant that he was aware of the possibility of approaching Beatrice, it seemed an absolute necessity of his existence to do so. It mattered not whether she were angel or demon; he was irrevocably within her sphere, and must obey the law that whirled him onward, in ever-lessening circles, towards a result which he did not attempt to foreshadow; and yet, strange to say, there came across him a sudden doubt whether this intense interest on his part were not delusory; whether it were really of so deep and positive a nature as to justify him in now thrusting himself into an incalculable position; whether it were not merely the fantasy of a young man's brain, only slightly or not at all connected with his heart.

He paused, hesitated, turned half about, but again went on. His withered guide led him along several obscure passages, and finally undid a door, through which, as it was opened, there came the sight and sound of rustling leaves, with the broken sunshine glimmering among them. Giovanni stepped forth, and, forcing himself through the entanglement of a shrub that wreathed its

Snatch – *Grab*
Smirk – *Grin*
Grotesque – *Incongruous*
Intrigue – *Plotting*

tendrils over the hidden entrance, stood beneath his own window in the open area of Dr. Rappaccini's garden.

How often is it the case that, when impossibilities have come to pass and dreams have condensed their misty substance into tangible realities, we find ourselves calm, and even coldly self-possessed, amid circumstances which it would have been a delirium of joy or agony to anticipate! Fate delights to thwart us thus. Passion will choose his own time to rush upon the scene, and lingers sluggishly behind when an appropriate adjustment of events would seem to summon his appearance. So was it now with Giovanni. Day after day his pulses had throbbed with feverish blood at the improbable idea of an interview with Beatrice, and of standing with her, face to face, in this very garden, basking in the Oriental sunshine of her beauty, and snatching from her full gaze the mystery which he deemed the riddle of his own existence. But now there was a singular and untimely equanimity within his breast. He threw a glance around the garden to discover if Beatrice or her father were present, and, perceiving that he was alone, began a critical observation of the plants.

The aspect of one and all of them dissatisfied him; their gorgeousness seemed fierce, passionate, and even unnatural. There was hardly an individual shrub which a wanderer, straying by himself through a forest, would not have been startled to find growing wild, as if an unearthly face had glared at him out of the thicket. Several also would have shocked a delicate instinct by an appearance of artificialness indicating that there had been such commixture, and, as it were, adultery, of various vegetable species, that the production was no longer of God's making, but the monstrous offspring of man's depraved fancy, glowing with only an evil mockery of beauty. They were probably the result of experiment, which in one or two cases had succeeded in mingling plants individually lovely into a compound possessing the questionable and ominous character that distinguished the whole growth of the garden. In fine, Giovanni recognized but two or three plants in the collection, and those of a kind that he well knew to be poisonous. While busy with these contemplations he heard the rustling of a silken garment, and, turning, beheld Beatrice emerging from beneath the sculptured portal.

Giovanni had not considered with himself what should be his deportment; whether he should apologize for his intrusion into the garden, or assume that he was there with the privities at

Suspicion – *Doubt*
Restrain – *Confine*
Irrevocable
– *Binding*
Delirium – *Fever*
Equanimity –
Composure

least, if not by the desire, of Dr. Rappaccini or his daughter; but Beatrice's manner placed him at his ease, though leaving him still in doubt by what agency he had gained admittance. She came lightly along the path and met him near the broken fountain. There was surprise in her face, but brightened by a simple and kind expression of pleasure.

"You are a connoisseur in flowers, signor," said Beatrice, with a smile, alluding to the bouquet which he had flung her from the window. "It is no marvel, therefore, if the sight of my father's rare collection has tempted you to take a nearer view. If he were here, he could tell you many strange and interesting facts as to the nature and habits of these shrubs; for he has spent a lifetime in such studies, and this garden is his world."

"And yourself, lady," observed Giovanni, "if fame says true, -- you likewise are deeply skilled in the virtues indicated by these rich blossoms and these spicy perfumes. Would you deign to be my instructress, I should prove an apter scholar than if taught by Signor Rappaccini himself."

"Are there such idle rumors?" asked Beatrice, with the music of a pleasant laugh. "Do people say that I am skilled in my father's science of plants? What a jest is there! No; though I have grown up among these flowers, I know no more of them than their hues and perfume; and sometimes methinks I would fain rid myself of even that small knowledge. There are many flowers here, and those not the least brilliant, that shock and offend me when they meet my eye. But pray, signor, do not believe these stories about my science. Believe nothing of me save what you see with your own eyes."

"And must I believe all that I have seen with my own eyes?" asked Giovanni, pointedly, while the recollection of former scenes made him shrink. "No, signora; you demand too little of me. Bid me believe nothing save what comes from your own lips."

It would appear that Beatrice understood him. There came a deep flush to her cheek; but she looked full into Giovanni's eyes, and responded to his gaze of uneasy suspicion with a queen-like haughtiness.

"I do so bid you, signor," she replied. "Forget whatever you may have fancied in regard to me. If true to the outward senses, still it may be false in its essence; but the words of Beatrice Rappaccini's lips are true from the depths of the heart outward. Those you may believe."

Instinct – *Nature*
Offspring – *Descendants*
Mingle – *Circulate*
Intrusion – *Interruption*
Fame – *Celebrity*

A fervor glowed in her whole aspect and beamed upon Giovanni's consciousness like the light of truth itself; but while she spoke there was a fragrance in the atmosphere around her, rich and delightful, though evanescent, yet which the young man, from an indefinable reluctance, scarcely dared to draw into his lungs. It might be the odor of the flowers. Could it be Beatrice's breath, which thus embalmed her words with a strange richness, as if by steeping them in her heart? A faintness passed like a shadow over Giovanni and flitted away; he seemed to gaze through the beautiful girl's eyes into her transparent soul, and felt no more doubt or fear.

The tinge of passion that had colored Beatrice's manner vanished; she became gay, and appeared to derive a pure delight from her communion with the youth not unlike what the maiden of a lonely island might have felt conversing with a voyager from the civilized world. Evidently her experience of life had been confined within the limits of that garden. She talked now about matters as simple as the daylight or summer clouds, and now asked questions in reference to the city, or Giovanni's distant home, his friends, his mother, and his sisters -- questions indicating such seclusion, and such lack of familiarity with modes and forms, that Giovanni responded as if to an infant. Her spirit gushed out before him like a fresh rill that was just catching its first glimpse of the sunlight and wondering at the reflections of earth and sky which were flung into its bosom. There came thoughts, too, from a deep source, and fantasies of a gem-like brilliancy, as if diamonds and rubies sparkled upward among the bubbles of the fountain. Ever and anon there gleamed across the young man's mind a sense of wonder that he should be walking side by side with the being who had so wrought upon his imagination, whom he had idealized in such hues of terror, in whom he had positively witnessed such manifestations of dreadful attributes, -- that he should be conversing with Beatrice like a brother, and should find her so human and so maiden-like. But such reflections were only momentary; the effect of her character was too real not to make itself familiar at once.

In this free intercourse they had strayed through the garden, and now, after many turns among its avenues, were come to the shattered fountain, beside which grew the magnificent shrub, with its treasury of glowing blossoms. A fragrance was diffused from it which Giovanni recognized as identical with that which he had attributed to Beatrice's breath, but incomparably more powerful. As her eyes fell upon it, Giovanni beheld her press her hand to her bosom as if her heart were throbbing suddenly and painfully.

"For the first time in my life," murmured she, addressing the shrub, "I had forgotten thee."

"I remember, signora," said Giovanni, "that you once promised to reward me with one of these living gems for the bouquet which I had the happy boldness to fling to your feet. Permit me now to pluck it as a memorial of this interview."

He made a step towards the shrub with extended hand; but Beatrice darted forward, uttering a shriek that went through his heart like a dagger. She caught his hand and drew it back with the whole force of her slender figure. Giovanni felt her touch thrilling through his fibers. "Touch it not!" exclaimed she, in a voice of agony. "Not for thy life! It is fatal!"

Then, hiding her face, she fled from him and vanished beneath the sculptured portal. As Giovanni followed her with his eyes, he beheld the emaciated figure and pale intelligence of Dr. Rappaccini, who had been watching the scene, he knew not how long, within the shadow of the entrance.

No sooner was Guasconti alone in his chamber than the image of Beatrice came back to his passionate musings, invested with all the witchery that had been gathering around it ever since his first glimpse of her, and now likewise imbued with a tender warmth of girlish womanhood. She was human; her nature was endowed with all gentle and feminine qualities; she was worthiest to be worshipped; she was capable, surely, on her part, of the height and heroism of love. Those tokens which he had hitherto considered as proofs of a frightful peculiarity in her physical and moral system were now either forgotten, or, by the subtle sophistry of passion transmitted into a golden crown of enchantment, rendering Beatrice the more admirable by so much as she was the more unique. Whatever had looked ugly was now beautiful; or, if incapable of such a change, it stole away and hid itself among those shapeless half ideas which throng the dim region beyond the daylight of our perfect consciousness. Thus did he spend the night, nor fell asleep until the dawn had begun to awake the slumbering flowers in Dr. Rappaccini's garden, whither Giovanni's dreams doubtless led him. Up rose the sun in his due season, and, flinging his beams

Seclusion – *Isolation*
Dreadful – *Terrible*
Utter – *Absolute*
Fatal – *Deadly*

upon the young man's eyelids, awoke him to a sense of pain. When thoroughly aroused, he became sensible of a burning and tingling agony in his hand -- in his right hand -- the very hand which Beatrice had grasped in her own when he was on the point of plucking one of the gem-like flowers. On the back of that hand there was now a purple print like that of four small fingers, and the likeness of a slender thumb upon his wrist.

Oh, how stubbornly does love, -- or even that cunning semblance of love which flourishes in the imagination, but strikes no depth of root into the heart, -- how stubbornly does it hold its faith until the moment comes when it is doomed to vanish into thin mist! Giovanni wrapped a handkerchief about his hand and wondered what evil thing had stung him, and soon forgot his pain in a reverie of Beatrice.

After the first interview, a second was in the inevitable course of what we call fate. A third; a fourth; and a meeting with Beatrice in the garden was no longer an incident in Giovanni's daily life, but the whole space in which he might be said to live; for the anticipation and memory of that ecstatic hour made up the remainder. Nor was it otherwise with the daughter of Rappaccini. She watched for the youth's appearance, and flew to his side with confidence as unreserved as if they had been playmates from early infancy -- as if they were such playmates still. If, by any unwonted chance, he failed to come at the appointed moment, she stood beneath the window and sent up the rich sweetness of her tones to float around him in his chamber and echo and reverberate throughout his heart: "Giovanni! Giovanni! Why tarriest thou? Come down!" And down he hastened into that Eden of poisonous flowers.

But, with all this intimate familiarity, there was still a reserve in Beatrice's demeanor, so rigidly and invariably sustained that the idea of infringing it scarcely occurred to his imagination. By all appreciable signs, they loved; they had looked love with eyes that conveyed the holy secret from the depths of one soul into the depths of the other, as if it were too sacred to be whispered by the way; they had even spoken love in those gushes of passion when their spirits darted forth in articulated breath like tongues of long-hidden flame; and yet there had been no seal of lips, no clasp of hands, nor any slightest caress such as love claims and hallows. He had never

Glimpse – *Sight*
peculiar – *odd*
render – *reduce*
Agony – *Anguish*
vanish – *disappear*

touched one of the gleaming ringlets of her hair; her garment -- so marked was the physical barrier between them -- had never been waved against him by a breeze. On the few occasions when Giovanni had seemed tempted to overstep the limit, Beatrice grew so sad, so stern, and withal wore such a look of desolate separation, shuddering at itself, that not a spoken word was requisite to repel him. At such times he was startled at the horrible suspicions that rose, monster-like, out of the caverns of his heart and stared him in the face; his love grew thin and faint as the morning mist, his doubts alone had substance. But, when Beatrice's face brightened again after the momentary shadow, she was transformed at once from the mysterious, questionable being whom he had watched with so much awe and horror; she was now the beautiful and unsophisticated girl whom he felt that his spirit knew with a certainty beyond all other knowledge.

A considerable time had now passed since Giovanni's last meeting with Baglioni. One morning, however, he was disagreeably surprised by a visit from the professor, whom he had scarcely thought of for whole weeks, and would willingly have forgotten still longer. Given up as he had long been to a pervading excitement, he could tolerate no companions except upon condition of their perfect sympathy with his present state of feeling. Such sympathy was not to be expected from Professor Baglioni.

The visitor chatted carelessly for a few moments about the gossip of the city and the university, and then took up another topic.

"I have been reading an old classic author lately," said he, "and met with a story that strangely interested me. Possibly you may remember it. It is of an Indian prince, who sent a beautiful woman as a present to Alexander the Great. She was as lovely as the dawn and gorgeous as the sunset; but what especially distinguished her was a certain rich perfume in her breath -- richer than a garden of Persian roses. Alexander, as was natural to a youthful conqueror, fell in love at first sight with this magnificent stranger; but a certain sage physician, happening to be present, discovered a terrible secret with regard to her."

"And what was that?" asked Giovanni, turning his eyes downward to avoid those of the professor "That this lovely woman," continued Baglioni, with emphasis, "had been nourished with poisons from her birth upward, until her whole nature was

Demeanor – *Manner*
Desolate – *Deserted*
repel – *deter*
momentary – *temporary*
awe – *wonder*

so imbued with them that she herself had become the deadliest poison in existence. Poison was her element of life. With that rich perfume of her breath she blasted the very air. Her love would have been poison -- her embrace death. Is not this a marvellous tale?"

"A childish fable," answered Giovanni, nervously starting from his chair. "I marvel how your worship finds time to read such nonsense among your graver studies."

"By the by," said the professor, looking uneasily about him, "what singular fragrance is this in your apartment? Is it the perfume of your gloves? It is faint, but delicious; and yet, after all, by no means agreeable. Were I to breathe it long, methinks it would make me ill. It is like the breath of a flower; but I see no flowers in the chamber."

"Nor are there any," replied Giovanni, who had turned pale as the professor spoke; "nor, I think, is there any fragrance except in your worship's imagination. Odors, being a sort of element combined of the sensual and the spiritual, are apt to deceive us in this manner. The recollection of a perfume, the bare idea of it, may easily be mistaken for a present reality."

"Ay, but my sober imagination does not often play such tricks," said Baglioni; "and, were I to fancy any kind of odor, it would be that of some vile apothecary drug, wherewith my fingers are likely enough to be imbued. Our worshipful friend Rappaccini, as I have heard, tinctures his medicaments with odors richer than those of Araby. Doubtless, likewise, the fair and learned Signora Beatrice would minister to her patients with draughts as sweet as a maiden's breath; but woe to him that sips them!"

Giovanni's face evinced many contending emotions. The tone in which the professor alluded to the pure and lovely daughter of Rappaccini was a torture to his soul; and yet the intimation of a view of her character opposite to his own, gave instantaneous distinctness to a thousand dim suspicions, which now grinned at him like so many demons. But he strove hard to quell them and to respond to Baglioni with a true lover's perfect faith.

Pervading –
Permeating
Conqueror
– *Defeater*
Magnificent – *Superb*
Fable – *Tale*

"Signor professor," said he, "you were my father's friend; perchance, too, it is your purpose to act a friendly part towards his son. I would fain feel nothing towards you save respect and deference; but I pray you to observe, signor, that there is one subject on which we must not speak. You know not the Signora

Beatrice. You cannot, therefore, estimate the wrong -- the blasphemy, I may even say -- that is offered to her character by a light or injurious word."

"Giovanni! My poor Giovanni!" answered the professor, with a calm expression of pity, "I know this wretched girl far better than yourself. You shall hear the truth in respect to the poisoner Rappaccini and his poisonous daughter; yes, poisonous as she is beautiful. Listen; for, even should you do violence to my gray hairs, it shall not silence me. That old fable of the Indian woman has become a truth by the deep and deadly science of Rappaccini and in the person of the lovely Beatrice."

Giovanni groaned and hid his face.

"Her father," continued Baglioni, "was not restrained by natural affection from offering up his child in this horrible manner as the victim of his insane zeal for science; for, let us do him justice, he is as true a man of science as ever distilled his own heart in an alembic. What, then, will be your fate? Beyond a doubt you are selected as the material of some new experiment. Perhaps the result is to be death; perhaps a fate more awful still. Rappaccini, with what he calls the interest of science before his eyes, will hesitate at nothing."

"It is a dream," muttered Giovanni to himself; "surely it is a dream."

"But," resumed the professor, "be of good cheer, son of my friend. It is not yet too late for the rescue. Possibly we may even succeed in bringing back this miserable child within the limits of ordinary nature, from which her father's madness has estranged her. Behold this little silver vase! It was wrought by the hands of the renowned Benvenuto Cellini, and is well worthy to be a love gift to the fairest dame in Italy. But its contents are invaluable. One little sip of this antidote would have rendered the most virulent poisons of the Borgias innocuous. Doubt not that it will be as efficacious against those of Rappaccini. Bestow the vase, and the precious liquid within it, on your Beatrice, and hopefully await the result."

Baglioni laid a small, exquisitely wrought silver vial on the table and withdrew, leaving what he had said to produce its effect upon the young man's mind.

"We will thwart Rappaccini yet," thought he, chuckling to himself, as he descended the stairs; "but, let us confess the truth of him, he is a wonderful man -- a wonderful man indeed;

Deceive – *Cheat*
Evince – *Show*
Quell – *Suppress*
Deference
– *Rmespect*

a vile empiric, however, in his practice, and therefore not to be tolerated by those who respect the good old rules of the medical profession."

Throughout Giovanni's whole acquaintance with Beatrice, he had occasionally, as we have said, been haunted by dark surmises as to her character; yet so thoroughly had she made herself felt by him as a simple, natural, most affectionate, and guileless creature, that the image now held up by Professor Baglioni looked as strange and incredible as if it were not in accordance with his own original conception. True, there were ugly recollections connected with his first glimpses of the beautiful girl; he could not quite forget the bouquet that withered in her grasp, and the insect that perished amid the sunny air, by no ostensible agency save the fragrance of her breath. These incidents, however, dissolving in the pure light of her character, had no longer the efficacy of facts, but were acknowledged as mistaken fantasies, by whatever testimony of the senses they might appear to be substantiated. There is something truer and more real than what we can see with the eyes and touch with the finger. On such better evidence had Giovanni founded his confidence in Beatrice, though rather by the necessary force of her high attributes than by any deep and generous faith on his part. But now his spirit was incapable of sustaining itself at the height to which the early enthusiasm of passion had exalted it; he fell down, grovelling among earthly doubts, and defiled therewith the pure whiteness of Beatrice's image. Not that he gave her up; he did but distrust. He resolved to institute some decisive test that should satisfy him, once for all, whether there were those dreadful peculiarities in her physical nature which could not be supposed to exist without some corresponding monstrosity of soul. His eyes, gazing down afar, might have deceived him as to the lizard, the insect, and the flowers; but if he could witness, at the distance of a few paces, the sudden blight of one fresh and healthful flower in Beatrice's hand, there would be room for no further question. With this idea he hastened to the florist's and purchased a bouquet that was still gemmed with the morning dew drops.

It was now the customary hour of his daily interview with Beatrice. Before descending into the garden, Giovanni failed not to look at his figure in the mirror, -- a vanity to be expected in a beautiful young man, yet, as displaying itself at that troubled and feverish moment, the token of a certain shallowness of feeling and insincerity of character. He did gaze, however, and said

Estrange – *To separate and live apart*
Virulent – *Infectious*
Innocuous – *Inoffensive*
Thwart – *Ruin*
Ostensible – *Apparent, Seeming*

to himself that his features had never before possessed so rich a grace, nor his eyes such vivacity, nor his cheeks so warm a hue of super abundant life.

"At least," thought he, "her poison has not yet insinuated itself into my system. I am no flower to perish in her grasp."

With that thought he turned his eyes on the bouquet, which he had never once laid aside from his hand. A thrill of indefinable horror shot through his frame on perceiving that those dewy flowers were already beginning to droop; they wore the aspect of things that had been fresh and lovely yesterday. Giovanni grew white as marble, and stood motionless before the mirror, staring at his own reflection there as at the likeness of something frightful. He remembered Baglioni's remark about the fragrance that seemed to pervade the chamber. It must have been the poison in his breath! Then he shuddered -- shuddered at himself. Recovering from his stupor, he began to watch with curious eye a spider that was busily at work hanging its web from the antique cornice of the apartment, crossing and re-crossing the artful system of interwoven lines -- as vigorous and active a spider as ever dangled from an old ceiling. Giovanni bent towards the insect, and emitted a deep, long breath. The spider suddenly ceased its toil; the web vibrated with a tremor originating in the body of the small artisan. Again Giovanni sent forth a breath, deeper, longer, and imbued with a venomous feeling out of his heart. He knew not whether he were wicked, or only desperate. The spider made a convulsive gripe with his limbs and hung dead across the window.

"Accursed! Accursed!" muttered Giovanni, addressing himself. "Hast thou grown so poisonous that this deadly insect perishes by thy breath?"

At that moment a rich, sweet voice came floating up from the garden "Giovanni! Giovanni! It is past the hour! Why tarriest thou? Come down!"

"Yes," muttered Giovanni again. "She is the only being whom my breath may not slay! Would that it might!"

He rushed down, and in an instant was standing before the bright and loving eyes of Beatrice. A moment ago his wrath and despair had been so fierce that he could have desired nothing so much as to wither her by a glance; but with her actual presence there came influences which had too real an existence to be at once shaken off. Recollections of the delicate and benign power

Testimony – *Demonstration*
Vanity – *Pride*
Gaze – *Look*
Insinuated – *Implied, Suggested*
Horror – *Dismay*

of her feminine nature, which had so often enveloped him in a religious calm; recollections of many a holy and passionate out-gush of her heart, when the pure fountain had been unsealed from its depths and made visible in its transparency to his mental eye; recollections which, had Giovanni known how to estimate them, would have assured him that all this ugly mystery was but an earthly illusion, and that, whatever mist of evil might seem to have gathered over her, the real Beatrice was a heavenly angel. Incapable as he was of such high faith, still her presence had not utterly lost its magic. Giovanni's rage was quelled into an aspect of sullen insensibility. Beatrice, with a quick spiritual sense, immediately felt that there was a gulf of blackness between them which neither he nor she could pass. They walked on together, sad and silent, and came thus to the marble fountain and to its pool of water on the ground, in the midst of which grew the shrub that bore gem-like blossoms. Giovanni was affrighted at the eager enjoyment -- the appetite, as it were -- with which he found himself inhaling the fragrance of the flowers.

"Beatrice," asked he, abruptly, "whence came this shrub?"

"My father created it," answered she, with simplicity.

"Created it! Created it!" repeated Giovanni. "What mean you, Beatrice?"

"He is a man fearfully acquainted with the secrets of Nature," replied Beatrice; "and, at the hour when I first drew breath, this plant sprang from the soil, the offspring of his science, of his intellect, while I was but his earthly child. Approach it not!" continued she, observing with terror that Giovanni was drawing nearer to the shrub. "It has qualities that you little dream of. But I, dearest Giovanni, -- I grew up and blossomed with the plant and was nourished with its breath. It was my sister, and I loved it with a human affection; for, alas! -- hast thou not suspected it? -- there was an awful doom."

Here Giovanni frowned so darkly upon her that Beatrice paused and trembled. But her faith in his tenderness reassured her, and made her blush that she had doubted for an instant. "There was an awful doom," she continued, "the effect of my father's fatal love of science, which estranged me from all society of my kind. Until Heaven sent thee, dearest Giovanni, oh, how lonely was thy poor Beatrice!"

"Was it a hard doom?" asked Giovanni, fixing his eyes upon her.

Pervade – *Permeate*
Stupor – *Lethargy*
Wrath – *Anger*
Benign – *Kind*

"Only of late have I known how hard it was," answered she, tenderly. "Oh, yes; but my heart was torpid, and therefore quiet."

Giovanni's rage broke forth from his sullen gloom like a lightning flash out of a dark cloud.

"Accursed one!" cried he, with venomous scorn and anger. "And, finding thy solitude wearisome, thou hast severed me likewise from all the warmth of life and enticed me into thy region of unspeakable horror!"

"Giovanni!" exclaimed Beatrice, turning her large bright eyes upon his face. The force of his words had not found its way into her mind; she was merely thunderstruck.

"Yes, poisonous thing!" repeated Giovanni, beside himself with passion. "Thou hast done it! Thou hast blasted me! Thou hast filled my veins with poison! Thou hast made me as hateful, as ugly, as loathsome and deadly a creature as thyself -- a world's wonder of hideous monstrosity! Now, if our breath be happily as fatal to ourselves as to all others, let us join our lips in one kiss of unutterable hatred, and so die!"

"What has befallen me?" murmured Beatrice, with a low moan out of her heart. "Holy Virgin, pity me, a poor heart-broken child!"

"Thou, -- dost thou pray?" cried Giovanni, still with the same fiendish scorn. "Thy very prayers, as they come from thy lips, taint the atmosphere with death. Yes, yes; let us pray! Let us to church and dip our fingers in the holy water at the portal! They that come after us will perish as by a pestilence! Let us sign crosses in the air! It will be scattering curses abroad in the likeness of holy symbols!"

"Giovanni," said Beatrice, calmly, for her grief was beyond passion, "why dost thou join thyself with me thus in those terrible words? I, it is true, am the horrible thing thou namest me. But thou, -- what hast thou to do, save with one other shudder at my hideous misery to go forth out of the garden and mingle with thy race, and forget there ever crawled on earth such a monster as poor Beatrice?"

"Dost thou pretend ignorance?" asked Giovanni, scowling upon her. "Behold! This power have I gained from the pure daughter of Rappaccini.

Abrupt – *Sudden*
Tremble – *Shake*
Torpid – *Sluggish*
Scorn – *Contempt*

There was a swarm of summer insects flitting through the air in search of the food promised by the flower odors of the fatal garden. They circled round Giovanni's head, and were evidently attracted towards him by the same influence which had drawn them for an instant within the sphere of several of the shrubs. He sent forth a breath among them, and smiled bitterly at Beatrice as at least a score of the insects fell dead upon the ground.

"I see it! I see it!" shrieked Beatrice. "It is my father's fatal science! No, no, Giovanni; it was not I! Never! Never! I dreamed only to love thee and be with thee a little time, and so to let thee pass away, leaving but thine image in mine heart; for, Giovanni, believe it, though my body be nourished with poison, my spirit is God's creature, and craves love as its daily food. But my father, -- he has united us in this fearful sympathy. Yes; spurn me, tread upon me, kill me! Oh, what is death after such words as thine? But it was not I. Not for a world of bliss would I have done it."

Giovanni's passion had exhausted itself in its outburst from his lips. There now came across him a sense, mournful, and not without tenderness, of the intimate and peculiar relationship between Beatrice and himself. They stood, as it were, in an utter solitude, which would be made none the less solitary by the densest throng of human life. Ought not, then, the desert of humanity around them to press this insulated pair closer together? If they should be cruel to one another, who was there to be kind to them? Besides, thought Giovanni, might there not still be a hope of his returning within the limits of ordinary nature, and leading Beatrice, the redeemed Beatrice, by the hand? O, weak, and selfish, and unworthy spirit, that could dream of an earthly union and earthly happiness as possible, after such deep love had been so bitterly wronged as was Beatrice's love by Giovanni's blighting words! No, no; there could be no such hope. She must pass heavily, with that broken heart, across the borders of Time -- she must bathe her hurts in some fount of paradise, and forget her grief in the light of immortality, and there be well.

But Giovanni did not know it.

"Dear Beatrice," said he, approaching her, while she shrank away as always at his approach, but now with a different impulse, "dearest Beatrice, our fate is not yet so desperate. Behold! There is a medicine, potent, as a wise physician has assured me, and almost divine in its efficacy. It is composed of ingredients the

Befallen – *Happened*
Moan – *Sigh*
Scowling – *Angry*
Fatal – *Deadly*

most opposite to those by which thy awful father has brought this calamity upon thee and me. It is distilled of blessed herbs. Shall we not quaff it together, and thus be purified from evil?"

"Give it to me!" said Beatrice, extending her hand to receive the little silver vial which Giovanni took from his bosom. She added, with a peculiar emphasis, "I will drink; but do thou await the result."

She put Baglioni's antidote to her lips; and, at the same moment, the figure of Rappaccini emerged from the portal and came slowly towards the marble fountain. As he drew near, the pale man of science seemed to gaze with a triumphant expression at the beautiful youth and maiden, as might an artist who should spend his life in achieving a picture or a group of statuary and finally be satisfied with his success. He paused; his bent form grew erect with conscious power; he spread out his hands over them in the attitude of a father imploring a blessing upon his children; but those were the same hands that had thrown poison into the stream of their lives. Giovanni trembled. Beatrice shuddered nervously, and pressed her hand upon her heart.

"My daughter," said Rappaccini, "thou art no longer lonely in the world. Pluck one of those precious gems from thy sister shrub and bid thy bridegroom wear it in his bosom. It will not harm him now. My science and the sympathy between thee and him have so wrought within his system that he now stands apart from common men, as thou dost, daughter of my pride and triumph, from ordinary women. Pass on, then, through the world, most dear to one another and dreadful to all besides!"

"My father," said Beatrice, feebly, -- and still as she spoke she kept her hand upon her heart, --"wherefore didst thou inflict this miserable doom upon thy child?"

"Miserable!" exclaimed Rappaccini. "What mean you, foolish girl? Dost thou deem it misery to be endowed with marvellous gifts against which no power nor strength could avail an enemy -- misery, to be able to quell the mightiest with a breath -- misery, to be as terrible as thou art beautiful? Wouldst thou, then, have preferred the condition of a weak woman, exposed to all evil and capable of none?"

"I would fain have been loved, not feared," murmured Beatrice, sinking down upon the ground. "But now it matters not. I am going, father, where the evil which thou hast striven to

Outburst – *Outpouring*
unworthy – *Undeserving*
Awful – *Dreadful*
Antidote – *Cure*

mingle with my being will pass away like a dream like the fragrance of these poisonous flowers, which will no longer taint my breath among the flowers of Eden. Farewell, Giovanni! Thy words of hatred are like lead within my heart; but they, too, will fall away as I ascend. Oh, was there not, from the first, more poison in thy nature than in mine?"

To Beatrice, -- so radically had her earthly part been wrought upon by Rappaccini's skill, -- as poison had been life, so the powerful antidote was death; and thus the poor victim of man's ingenuity and of thwarted nature, and of the fatality that attends all such efforts of perverted wisdom, perished there, at the feet of her father and Giovanni. Just at that moment Professor Pietro Baglioni looked forth from the window, and called loudly, in a tone of triumph mixed with horror, to the thunder-stricken man of science, "Rappaccini! Rappaccini! And is *this* the upshot of your experiment!"

Food For Thought

The story has a tragic end as the antidote that Giovanni brings for his beloved, Beatrice kills her. How do you think Beatrice's father would have reacted to all this? Answer in your own words.

An Understanding

Q. 1. Who was Beatrice Rappaccini? How did she become poisonous?
Ans. _____
_____
_____
_____
_____

Q. 2. Who was Giovanni Guasconti? How did he fall in love with Beatrice Rappaccini?
Ans. _____

_____
_____
_____

Q. 3. What does Giovanni do when he discovers that he himself has become poisonous?
Ans. _____
_____
_____
_____
_____

Q. 4. Giovanni brings a powerful antidote to Beatrice so that they can be together forever, but what happens at the end?
Ans. _____
_____
_____
_____
_____

Thomas Hardy

Born on June 2, 1840

Died on January 11, 1928

Notable Works: *The Poor Man and the Lady, Desperate Remedies* and *Under the Greenwood Tree, A Pair of Blue Eyes, Far from the Madding Crowd, The Return of the Native , The Mayor of Casterbridge, Tess of the d'Urbervilles, Collected Poems,* etc.

Honour: *Order of Merit (OM)*

Early Life

Thomas Hardy, recipient of the *Order of Merit (OM)* was born on June 2, 1840 – an English novelist and poet. While his works typically belong to the Naturalism movement, several poems display elements of the previous Romantic and Enlightenment periods of literature, such as his fascination with the supernatural.

Thomas Hardy was born in Upper Bockhampton, a hamlet in the parish of Stinsford to the east of Dorchester in Dorset, England in 1840. His father, Thomas worked as a stonemason and local builder. His mother, Jemima was well-read. She educated Thomas until he went to his first school at Bockhampton at the age of eight. For several years, he attended Mr. Last's Academy for Young Gentlemen in Dorchester. Here he learnt Latin and demonstrated academic potential.

However, a family of Hardy's social position lacked the means for a university education, and his formal education ended at the age of sixteen when he became apprenticed to James Hicks, a local architect. Hardy was trained as an architect in Dorchester before moving to London in 1862. There, he enrolled as a student at King's College, London. He won prizes from the Royal Institute of British Architects and the Architectural Association. Hardy never felt at home in London. He was acutely conscious of class divisions and his social inferiority. However, he was interested in social reform and was familiar with the works of John Stuart Mill. He was also introduced to the works of Charles Fourier and Auguste Comte during this period by his Dorset friend, Horace Moule. Five years later, concerned about his health, he returned to Dorset and decided to dedicate himself to writing.

Literary Works and Achievements

Hardy's first novel, *The Poor Man and the Lady*, completed by 1867, failed to find a publisher and Hardy destroyed the manuscript, so only parts of the novel remain. He was encouraged to try again by his mentor and friend, Victorian poet and novelist George Meredith. *Desperate Remedies* (1871) and *Under the Greenwood Tree* (1872) were published anonymously. In 1873, *A Pair of Blue Eyes*, a novel drawing on Hardy's courtship of his first wife, was not published under his own name. Some of his well-known works were: *Far from the Madding Crowd* (1874), *The Return of the Native* (1878), *The Mayor of Casterbridge* (1886), etc.

Although his poems were not initially as well received by his contemporaries as his novels were, *Hardy is now recognised as one of the greatest poets of the twentieth century*. In 1898, Hardy published his first volume of poetry, *Wessex Poems*, a collection of poems written over 30 years. Hardy claimed poetry as his first love, and after a great amount of negative criticism erupted from the publication of his novel, *Jude The Obscure*, His verse had a profound influence on later writers, notably Philip Larkin, who included many of Hardy's poems in the edition of the *Oxford Book of Twentieth Century English Verse* that Larkin edited in 1973.

Most of Hardy's poems, such as *Neutral Tones* and *A Broken Appointment*. Hardy sometimes wrote ironic poems, like *Ah, Are You Digging On My Grave*, Some, like *The Darkling Thrush* and *An August Midnight*, appear as poems in which the nature mentioned in them gives Hardy the inspiration to write. A few of Hardy's poems, such as *The Blinded Bird* display his love of the natural world and his firm stance against animal cruelty.

Writing Style

His compositions range in style from the three-volume epic closet drama, *The Dynasts* to shorter poems, such as *A Broken Appointment*. His compositions primarily deal with the themes of disappointment in love and life (which were also prominent themes in his novels), and mankind's long struggle against indifference to human suffering. Hardy was also immensely influenced by the Nature and its wonders and derived inspiration from it, particularly while writing poetry.

Later Years

Hardy became ill with pleurisy in December 1927 and died at Max Gate on January 11, 1928, having dictated his final poem to his wife on his deathbed. The cause of death was cited, on his death certificate, as "cardiac syncope", with "old age" given as a contributory factor. In the year of his death, Mrs Hardy published *The Early Life of Thomas Hardy*, 1841–1891: compiled largely from contemporary notes, letters, diaries and biographical memoranda, as well as from oral information in conversations extending over many years.

Trivia

In 1910, Hardy was awarded the **Order of Merit or OM**. The Order of Merit (French: Ordre du Mérite) is a dynastic order recognising distinguished service in the armed forces, science, art, literature, or for the promotion of culture established in 1902 by King Edward VII.

Destiny and a Blue Cloak

~Thomas Hardy

I

"**G**ood morning, Miss Lovill!" said the young man, in the free manner usual with him towards pretty and inexperienced country girls.

Agatha Pollin - the maiden addressed - instantly perceived how the mistake had arisen. Miss Lovill was the owner of a blue autumn wrapper, exceptionally gay for a village; and Agatha, in a spirit of emulation rather than originality, had purchased a similarly enviable article for herself, which she wore today for the first time. It may be mentioned that the two young women had ridden together from their homes to Maiden-Newton on this foggy September morning, Agatha prolonging her journey thence to Weymouth by train, and leaving her acquaintance at the former place. The remark was made to her on Weymouth esplanade.

Agatha was now about to reply very naturally, "I am not Miss Lovill," and she went so far as to turn up her face to him for the purpose, when he added, "I've been hoping to meet you. I have heard of your - well, I must say it - beauty, long ago, though I only came to Beaminster yesterday." Agatha bowed - her contradiction hung back - and they walked slowly along the esplanade together without speaking another word after the above point-blank remark of his. It was evident that her new friend could never have seen either herself or Miss Lovill except from a distance.

And Agatha trembled as well as bowed. This Miss Lovill - Frances Lovill - was of great and long renown as the beauty of Cloton village, near Beaminster. She was five and twenty and fully developed, while Agatha was only the niece of the miller of the same place, just nineteen, and of no repute as yet for comeliness, though she undoubtedly could boast of much. Now, as the speaker, Oswald Winwood, to be told that he had not lighted upon the true Helen, he would instantly apologize for his mistake and leave her side; contingency of no great matter but for one curious emotional circumstance - Agatha

Perceive – *Observe*
Esplanade – *Walkway*
Contradiction – *Illogicality*
Contingency – *Eventuality*

had already lost her heart to him. Only in secret had she acquired this interest in Winwood - by hearing much report of his talent and by watching him several times from a window; but she loved none the less in that she had discovered that Miss Lovill's desire to meet and talk with the same intellectual luminary was in a fair way of approaching the intensity of her own. We are never unbiased appraisers, even in love, and rivalry usually operates as a stimulant to esteem even while it is acting as an obstacle to opportunity. So it had been with Agatha in her talk to Miss Lovill that morning concerning Oswald Winwood.

The Weymouth season was almost at an end, and but few loungers were to be seen on the parades, particularly at this early hour. Agatha looked over the iridescent sea, from which the veil of mist was slowly rising, at the white cliffs on the left, now just beginning to gleam in a weak sunlight, at the one solitary yacht in the midst, and still delayed her explanation. Her companion went on,

"The mist is vanishing, look, and I think it will be fine, after all. Shall you stay in Weymouth the whole day?"

"No. I am going to Portland by the twelve o'clock steam boat. But I return here again at six to go home by the seven o'clock train."

"I go to Maiden Newton by the same train, and then to Beaminster by the carrier."

"So do I."

"Not, I suppose, to walk from Beaminster to Cloton at that time in the evening?"

"I shall be met by somebody - but it is only a mile, you know."

That is how it all began; the continuation it is not necessary to detail at length. Both being somewhat young and impulsive, social forms were not scrupulously attended to. She discovered him to be on board the steamer as it ploughed the emerald waves of Weymouth Bay, although he had wished her a formal good bye at the pier. He had altered his mind, he said, and thought that he would come to Portland, too. They returned by the same boat, walked the velvet sands till the train started, and entered a carriage together.

All this time, in the midst of her happiness, Agatha's conscience was somber with guiltiness at not having yet told

Intellectual –
Intelligent
Rivalry
– Competition
Vanish *– Disappear*
Alter *– Change*

him of his mistake. It was true that he had not more than once or twice called her by Miss Lovill's name since the first greeting in the morning; but he certainly was still under the impression that she was Frances Lovill. Yet she perceived that though he had been led to her by another's name, it was her own proper person that he was so rapidly getting to love, and Agatha's feminine insight suggested blissfully to her that the face belonging to the name would after this encounter have no power to drag him away from the face of the day's romance.

They reached Maiden-Newton at dusk, and went to the inn door, where stood the old-fashioned hooded van which was to take them to Beaminster. It was on the point of starting, and when they had mounted in front the old man at once drove up the long hill leading out of the village.

"This has been a charming experience to me, Miss Lovill," Oswald said, as they sat side by side. "Accidental meetings have a way of making themselves pleasant when contrived ones quite fail to do it."

It was absolutely necessary to confess this time, though all her bliss were at once destroyed.

"I am not really Miss Lovill!" she faltered.

"What! Not the young lady - and are you really not Frances Lovill?" he exclaimed, in surprise.

"O forgive me, Mr. Winwood! I have wanted so to tell you of your mistake; indeed I have, all day - but I couldn't - and it is so wicked and wrong of me! I am only poor Agatha Pollin, at the mill."

"But why couldn't you tell me?"

"Because I was afraid that if I did you would go away from me and not care for me any more, and I l-l-love you so dearly!"

The carrier being on foot beside the horse, the van being so dark, and Oswald's feelings being rather warm, he could not for his life avoid kissing her there and then.

"Well," he said, "it doesn't matter; you are yourself anyhow. It is you I like, and nobody else in the world - not the name. But, you know, I was really looking for Miss Lovill this morning. I saw the back of her head yesterday, and I have often heard how very good-looking she is. Ah! Suppose you had been she. I wonder--"

Blissfully
– *Supremely*
Charming – *Delightful*
Contrive – *Arrange*
Confess – *Admit*

He did not complete the sentence. The driver mounted again, touched the horse with the whip, and they jogged on.

"You forgive me?" she said.

"Entirely - absolutely - the reason justified everything. How strange that you should have been caring deeply for me, and I ignorant of it all the time!"

They descended into Beaminster and alighted, Oswald handing her down. They had not moved from the spot when another female figure also alighted, dropped her fare into the carrier's hand, and glided away.

"Who is that?" said Oswald to the carrier. "Why, I thought we were the only passengers!"

"What?" said the carrier, who was rather stupid.

"Who is that woman?"

"Miss Lovill, of Cloton. She altered her mind about staying at Beaminster, and is come home again." "Oh!" said Agatha, almost sinking to the earth. "She has heard it all. What shall I do, what shall I do?"

"Never mind it a bit," said Oswald.

II

The mill stood beside the village high road, from which it was separated by the stream, the latter forming also the boundary of the mill garden, orchard, and paddock on that side. A visitor crossed a little wood bridge embedded in oozy, aquatic growths, and found himself in a space where usually stood a wagon laden with sacks, surrounded by a number of bright-feathered fowls.

It was now, however, just dusk, but the mill was not closed, a stripe of light stretching as usual from the open door across the front, across the river, across the road, into the hedge beyond. On the bridge, which was aside from the line of light, a young man and girl stood talking together. Soon they moved a little way apart, and then it was apparent that their right hands were joined. In receding one from the other they began to swing their arms gently backward and forward between them.

Descended – *Sloped*
Alighted – *Landed*
Embedded – *Entrenched*
Apparent – *Seeming*

"Come a little way up the lane, Agatha, since it is the last time," he said. "I don't like parting here. You know your uncle does not object."

"He doesn't object because he knows nothing to object to," she whispered. And they both then contemplated the fine, stalwart figure of the said uncle, who could be seen moving about inside the mill, illuminated by the candle, and circumscribed by a faint halo of flour, and hindered by the whirr of the mill from hearing anything so gentle as lovers' talk.

Oswald had not relinquished her hand, and, submitting herself to a bondage she appeared to love better than freedom, Agatha followed him across the bridge, and they went down the lane engaged in the low, sad talk common to all such cases, interspersed with remarks peculiar to their own.

"It is nothing so fearful to contemplate," he said. "Many live there for years in a state of rude health, and return home in the same happy condition. So shall I."

"I hope you will."

"But aren't you glad I am going? It is better to do well in India than badly here. Say you are glad, dearest; it will fortify me when I am gone."

"I am glad," she murmured faintly. "I mean I am glad in my mind. I don't think that in my heart I am glad."

"Thanks to Macaulay, of honored memory, I have as good a chance as the best of them!" he said, with ardor. "What a great thing competitive examination is; it will put good men in good places, and make inferior men move lower down; all bureaucratic jobbery will be swept away."

"What's bureaucratic, Oswald?"

"Oh! That's what they call it, you know. It is - well, I don't exactly know what it is. I know this, that it is the name of what I hate, and that it isn't competitive examination."

"At any rate it is a very bad thing," she said, conclusively.

"Very bad, indeed; you may take my word for that."

Then the parting scene began, in the dark, under the heavy-headed trees which shut out sky and stars. "And since I shall be in London till the spring," he remarked, "the parting doesn't seem so bad - so all at once. Perhaps you may come to London before the spring, Agatha."

"I may, but I don't think I shall."

"We must hope on all the same. Then there will be the examination, and then I shall know my fate." "I hope you'll fail! - there, I've said it; I couldn't help it, Oswald!" she exclaimed, bursting out crying. "You would come home again then!"

Contemplate –
Anticipate
Stalwart – *Resolute*
Relinquish –
Surrender
Fortify – *Strengthen*

"How can you be so disheartening and wicked, Agatha! I-I didn't expect--"

"No, no; I don't wish it; I wish you to be best, top, very, very best!" she said. "I didn't mean the other; indeed, dear Oswald, I didn't. And will you be sure to come to me when you are rich? Sure to come?"

"If I'm on this earth I'll come home and marry you."

And then followed the good bye.

III

In the spring came the examination. One morning a newspaper directed by Oswald was placed in her hands, and she opened it to find it was a copy of the Times. In the middle of the sheet, in the most conspicuous place, in the excellent neighborhood of the leading articles, was a list of names, and the first on the list was Oswald Winwood. Attached to his name, as showing where he was educated, was the simple title of some obscure little academy, while underneath came public school and college men in shoals. Such a case occurs sometimes, and it occurred then.

How Agatha clapped her hands! For her selfish wish to have him in England at any price, even that of failure, had been but a paroxysm of the wretched parting, and was now quite extinct. Circumstances combined to hinder another meeting between them before his departure, and, accordingly, making up her mind to the inevitable in a way which would have done honour to an older head, she fixed her mental vision on that sunlit future - far away, yet always nearing - and contemplated its probabilities with a firm hope.

At length he had arrived in India, and now Agatha had only to work and wait; and the former made the latter more easy. In her spare hours she would wander about the river brinks and into the coppices and there weave thoughts of him by processes that young women understand so well. She kept a diary, and in this, since there were few events to chronicle in her daily life, she sketched the changes of the landscape, noted the arrival and departure of birds of passage, the times of storms and foul weather - all which information, being mixed up with her life and taking color from it, she sent as scraps in her letters to him, deriving most of her enjoyment in contemplating his.

Disheartening –
Intimidating
Conspicuous – *Visible*
Paroxysm –
Convulsion
Extinct – *Obsolete*

Oswald, on his part, corresponded very regularly. Knowing the days of the Indian mail, she would go at such times to meet the postman in early morning, and to her unvarying inquiry, "A letter for me?" it was seldom, indeed, that there came a disappointing answer. Thus the season passed, and Oswald told her he should be a judge some day, with many other details, which, in her mind, were viewed chiefly in their bearing on the grand consummation - that he was to come home and marry her.

Meanwhile, as the girl grew older and more womanly, the woman whose name she had once stolen for a day grew more of an old maid, and showed symptoms of fading. One day Agatha's uncle, who, though still a handsome man in the prime of his life was a widower with four children, to whom she acted the part of eldest sister, told Agatha that Frances Lovill was about to become his second wife.

"Well!" said Agatha, and thought, "What an end for a beauty!"

And yet it was all reasonable enough, notwithstanding that Miss Lovill might have looked a little higher. Agatha knew that this step would produce great alterations in the small household of Cloton Mill, and the idea of having as aunt and ruler the woman to whom she was in some sense indebted for a lover, affected Agatha with a slight thrill of dread. Yet nothing had ever been spoken between the two women to show that Frances had heard, much less resented, the explanation in the van on that night of the return from Weymouth.

IV

On a certain day old farmer Lovill called. He was of the same family as Frances, though their relationship was distant. A considerable business in corn had been done from time to time between miller and farmer, but the latter had seldom called at Pollin's house. He was a bachelor, or he would probably never have appeared in this history, and he was mostly full of a boyish merriment rare in one of his years. Today his business with the miller had been so imperative as to bring him in person, and it was evident from their talk in the mill that the matter was payment. Perhaps ten minutes had been spent in serious converse when the old farmer turned away from the door,

Contemplate –
Anticipate
Inquiry – *Investigation*
Resent – *To feel/ show displeasure*
Imperative –
Indispensable

and, without saying good morning, went towards the bridge. This was unusual for a man of his temperament.

He was an old man - really and fairly old - sixty-five years of age at least. He was not exactly feeble, but he found a stick useful when walking in a high wind. His eyes were not yet bleared, but in their corners was occasionally a moisture like majolica glaze - entirely absent in youth. His face was not shriveled, but there were unmistakable puckers in some places. And hence the old gentleman, unmarried, substantial, and cheery as he was, was not doted on by the young girls of Cloton as he had been by their mothers in former time. Each year his breast impended a little further over his toes, and his chin a little further over his breast, and in proportion as he turned down his nose to earth did pretty females turn up theirs at him. They might have liked him as a friend had he not shown the abnormal wish to be regarded as a lover. To Agatha Pollin this aged youth was positively distasteful.

It happened that at the hour of Mr. Lovill's visit Agatha was bending over the pool at the mill head, sousing some white fabric in the water. She was quite unconscious of the farmer's presence near her, and continued dipping and rinsing in the idlest phase possible to industry, until she remained quite still, holding the article under the water, and looking at her own reflection within it. The river, though gliding slowly, was yet so smooth that to the old man on the bridge she existed in duplicate - the pouting mouth, the little nose, the frizzed hair, the bit of blue ribbon, as they existed over the surface, being but a degree more distinct than the same features beneath.

"What a pretty maid!" said the old man to himself. He walked up the margin of the stream, and stood beside her.

"Oh!" said Agatha, starting with surprise. In her flurry she relinquished the article she had been rinsing, which slowly turned over and sank deeper, and made toward the hatch of the mill wheel.

"There - it will get into the wheel, and be torn to pieces!" she exclaimed.

"I'll fish it out with my stick, my dear," said Farmer Lovill, and kneeling cautiously down he began hooking and crooking with all his might. "What thing is it of much value?"

Feeble – *Weak*
Shrivelled
– *Shrunken*
Flurry – *Burst*
Relinquish –
Renounce

"Yes; it is my best one!" she said involuntarily.

"It - what is the it?"

"Only something - a piece of linen." Just then the farmer hooked the endangered article, and dragging it out, held it high on his walking stick - dripping, but safe.

"Why, it is a chemise!" he said.

The girl looked red, and instead of taking it from the end of the stick, turned away.

"Hee-hee!" laughed the ancient man. "Well, my dear, there's nothing to be ashamed of that I can see in owning to such a necessary and innocent article of clothing. There, I'll put it on the grass for you, and you shall take it when I am gone."

Then Farmer Lovill retired, lifting his fingers privately, to express amazement on a small scale, and murmuring, "What a nice young thing! Well, to be sure. Yes, a nice child - young woman rather indeed, a marriageable woman, come to that; of course she is."

The doting old person thought of the young one all this day in a way that the young one did not think of him. He thought so much about her, that in the evening, instead of going to bed, he hobbled privately out by the back door into the moonlight, crossed a field or two, and stood in the lane, looking at the mill - not more in the hope of getting a glimpse of the attractive girl inside than for the pleasure of realizing that she was there.

A light moved within, came nearer, and ascended. The staircase window was large, and he saw his goddess going up with a candle in her hand. This was indeed worth coming for. He feared he was seen by her as well, yet hoped otherwise in the interests of his passion, for she came and drew down the window blind, completely shutting out his gaze. The light vanished from this part, and reappeared in a window a little further on.

The lover drew nearer; this, then, was her bedroom. He rested vigorously upon his stick, and straightening his back nearly to a perpendicular, turned up his amorous face.

She came to the window, paused, then opened it.

"Bless its deary-eary heart! It is going to speak to me!" said the old man, moistening his lips, resting still more desperately

Endangered – *Threatened*
Glimpse – *Sight*
Vanish – *Disappear*
Vigorous – *Energetic*

upon his stick, and straightening himself yet an inch taller. "She saw me then!"

Agatha, however, made no sign; she was bent on a far different purpose. In a box on her window sill was a row of mignonette, which had been sadly neglected since her lover's departure, and she began to water it, as if inspired by a sudden recollection of its condition. She poured from her water jug slowly along the plants, and then, to her astonishment, discerned her elderly friend below.

"A rude old thing!" she murmured.

Directing the spout of the jug over the edge of the box, and looking in another direction that it might appear to be an accident, she allowed the stream to spatter down upon her admirer's face, neck, and shoulders, causing him to beat a quick retreat. Then Agatha serenely closed the window, and drew down that blind also.

"Ah! She did not see me; it was evident she did not, and I was mistaken!" said the trembling farmer, hastily wiping his face, and mopping out the rills trickling down within his shirt collar as far as he could get at them, which was by no means to their termination. "A pretty creature, and so innocent, too! Watering her flowers; how like a girl who is fond of flowers! I wish she had spoken, and I wish I was younger. Yes, I know what I'd do with the little mouse!" And the old gentleman tapped emotionally upon the ground with his stick.

V

"Agatha, I suppose you have heard the news from somebody else by this time?" said her Uncle Humphrey some two or three weeks later. "I mean what Farmer Lovill has been talking to me about."

"No, indeed" said Agatha.

"He wants to marry ye if you be willing."

"O, I never!" said Agatha with dismay. "That old man!"

"Old? He's hale and hearty; and what's more, a man very well to do. He'll make you a comfortable home, and dress ye up like a doll, and I'm sure you'll like that, or you 'aint a woman of woman born."

Amorous – *Ardent*
Serenely – *Calmly*
Evident – *Obvious*
Dismay –
Disappointment

"But it can't be, uncle! Other reasons--"

"What reasons?"

"Why, I've promised Oswald Winwood - years ago!"

"Promised Oswald Winwood years ago, have you?"

"Yes; surely you know it Uncle Humphrey. And we write to one another regularly."

"Well, I can just call to mind that ye are always scribbling and getting letters from somewhere. Let me see - where is he now? I quite forget."

"In India still. Is it possible that you don't know about him, and what a great man he's getting? There are paragraphs about him in our paper very often. The last was about some translation from Hindostani that he'd been making. And he's coming home for me."

"I very much question it. Lovill will marry you at once, he says."

"Indeed, he will not."

"Well, I don't want to force you to do anything against your will, Agatha, but this is how the matter stands. You know I am a little behind hand in my dealings with Lovill - nothing serious, you know, if he gives me time - but I want to be free of him quite in order to go to Australia."

"Australia!" "Yes. There's nothing to be done here. I don't know what business is coming to - can't think. But never mind that; this is the point: if you will marry Farmer Lovill, he offers to clear off the debt, and there will no longer be any delay about my own marriage; in short, away I can go. I mean to, and there's an end on't."

"What, and leave me at home alone?"

"Yes, but a married woman, of course. You see the children are getting big now. John is twelve and Nathaniel ten, and the girls are growing fast, and when I am married again I shall hardly want you to keep house for me - in fact, I must reduce our family as much as possible. So that if you could bring your mind to think of Farmer Lovill as a husband, why, 'twould be a great relief to me after having the trouble and expense of bringing you up. If I can in that way edge out of Lovill's debt I shall have a nice bit of money in hand."

"But Oswald will be richer even than Mr. Lovill," said Agatha, through her tears.

Debt – *Obligation*
Relief – *Comfort*
Expense
– *Expenditure*

"Yes, yes. But Oswald is not here, nor is he likely to be. How silly you be."

"But he will come, and soon, with his eleven hundred a year and all."

"I wish to Heaven he would. I'm sure he might have you."

"Now, you promise that, uncle, don't you?" she said, brightening. "If he comes with plenty of money before you want to leave, he shall marry me, and nobody else."

"Ay, if he comes. But, Agatha, no nonsense. Just think of what I've been telling you. And at any rate be civil to Farmer Lovill. If this man Winwood were here and asked for ye, and married ye, that would be a very different thing. I do mind now that I saw something about him and his doings in the papers; but he's a fine gentleman by this time, and won't think of stooping to a girl like you. So you'd better take the one who is ready; old men's darlings fare very well as the world goes. We shall be off in nine months, mind, that I've settled. And you must be a married woman afore that time, and wish us good bye upon your husband's arm."

"That old arm couldn't support me."

"And if you don't agree to have him, you'll take a couple of hundred pounds out of my pocket; you'll ruin my chances altogether - that's the long and the short of it."

Saying which the man turned his back upon her, and his footsteps became drowned in the rumble of the mill.

VI

Nothing so definite was said to her again on the matter for some time. The old yeoman hovered round her, but, knowing the result of the interview between Agatha and her uncle, he forbore to endanger his suit by precipitancy. But one afternoon he could not avoid saying, "Aggie, when may I speak to you upon a serious subject?"

"Next week," she replied, instantly.

He had not been prepared for such a ready answer, and it startled him almost as much as it pleased him. Had he known the cause of it his emotions might have been different. Agatha, with all the womanly strategy she was capable of, had written post-haste to Oswald after the conversation

Plenty – *Adequately*
Rumble – *Roar*
Hover – *Float*
Startle – *Surprise*

with her uncle, and told him of the dilemma. At the end of the present week his answer, if he replied with his customary punctuality, would be sure to come. Fortified with his letter she thought she could meet the old man. Oswald she did not doubt.

Nor had she any reason to. The letter came prompt to the day. It was short, tender, and to the point. Events had shaped themselves so fortunately that he was able to say he would return and marry her before the time named for the family's departure for Queensland.

She danced about for joy. But there was a postscript to the effect that she might as well keep this promise a secret for the present, if she conveniently could, that his intention might not become a public talk in Cloton. Agatha knew that he was a rising and aristocratic young man, and saw at once how proper this was.

So she met Mr. Lovill with a simple flat refusal, at which her uncle was extremely angry, and her disclosure to him afterward of the arrival of the letter went but a little way in pacifying him. Farmer Lovill would put in upon him for the debt, he said, unless she could manage to please him for a short time.

"I don't want to please him," said Agatha. "It is wrong to encourage him if I don't mean it."

"Will you behave towards him as the Parson advises you?"

The Parson! That was a new idea, and, from her uncle, unexpected.

"I will agree to what Mr. Davids advises about my mere daily behavior before Oswald comes, but nothing more," she said. "That is, I will if you know for certain that he's a good man, who fears God and keeps the commandments."

"Mr. Davids fears God, for sartin, for he never ventures to name Him outside the pulpit - and as for the commandments, 'tis knowed how he swore at the church restorers for taking them away from the chancel."

"Uncle, you always jest when I am serious."

"Well, well! At any rate his advice on a matter of this sort is good."

"How is it you think of referring me to him?" she asked, in perplexity; "you so often speak slightingly of him."

Dilemma
– *Quandary,*
Uncertainty
Aristocratic – *Noble*
Ventures –
Undertakings
Perplexity –
Puzzlement

"Oh well," said Humphrey, with a faintly perceptible desire to parry the question, "I have spoken roughly about him once now and then; but perhaps I was wrong. Will ye go?"

"Yes, I don't mind," she said, languidly.

When she reached the Vicar's study Agatha began her story with reserve, and said nothing about the correspondence with Oswald; yet an intense longing to find a friend and confidant led her to indulge in more feeling than she had intended, and as a finale she wept. The genial incumbent, however, remained quite cool, the secret being that his heart was involved a little in another direction - one, perhaps, not quite in harmony with Agatha's interests - of which more anon.

"So the difficulty is," he said to her, "how to behave in this trying time of waiting for Mr. Winwood, that you may please parties all round and give offence to none."

"Yes, Sir, that's it," sobbed Agatha, wondering how he could have realized her position so readily. "And uncle wants to go to Australia."

"One thing is certain," said the Vicar; "you must not hurt the feelings of Mr. Lovill. Wonderfully sensitive man - a man I respect much as a godly doer."

"Do you, Sir?"

"I do. His earnestness is remarkable."

"Yes, in courting."

"The cue is: treat Mr. Lovill gently-gently as a babe! Love opposed, especially an old man's, gets all the stronger. It is your policy to give him seeming encouragement, and so let his feelings expend themselves and die away."

"How am I to? To advise is so easy."

"Not by acting untruthfully, of course. You say your lover is sure to come back before your uncle leaves England?"

"I know he will."

"Then pacify old Mr. Lovill in this way: Tell him you'll marry him when your uncle wants to go, if Winwood doesn't come for you before that time. That will quite content Mr. Lovill, for he doesn't in the least expect Oswald to return, and you'll see that his persecution will cease at once." "Yes; I'll agree to it," said Agatha promptly.

Mr. Davids had refrained from adding that neither did he expect Oswald to come, and hence his advice. Agatha on

Languid
– *Unenergetic*
Confidant – *Friend*
Content – *Gratified*
Refrain – *To abstain/ curb*

her part too refrained from stating the good reasons she had for the contrary expectation, and hence her assent. Without the last letter perhaps even her faith would hardly have been bold enough to allow this palpable driving of her into a corner.

"It would be as well to write Mr. Lovill a little note, saying you agree to what I have advised," said the Parson evasively.

"I don't like writing."

"There's no harm. 'If Mr. Winwood doesn't come I'll marry you'. Poor Mr. Lovill will be content, thinking Oswald will not come; you will be content, knowing he will come; your uncle will be content being indifferent which of two rich men has you and relieves him of his difficulties. Then, if it's the will of Providence, you'll be left in peace. Here's a pen and ink; you can do it at once."

Thus tempted, Agatha wrote the note with a trembling hand. It really did seem upon the whole a nicely strategic thing to do in her present environed situation. Mr. Davids took the note with the air of a man who did not wish to take it in the least, and placed it on the mantle-piece.

"I'll send it down to him by one of the children," said Aggy, looking wistfully at her note with a little feeling that she should like to have it back again.

"Oh, no, it is not necessary," said her pleasant adviser. He had rung the bell; the servant now came, and the note was sent off in a trice.

When Agatha got into the open air again her confidence returned, and it was with a mischievous sense of enjoyment that she considered how she was duping her persecutors by keeping secret Oswald's intention of a speedy return. If they only knew what a firm foundation she had for her belief in what they all deemed but an improbable contingency, what a life they would lead her; how the old man would worry her uncle for payment, and what general confusion there would be. Mr. Davids' advice was very shrewd, she thought, and she was glad she had called upon him.

Old Lovill came that very afternoon. He was delighted, and danced a few bars of a hornpipe in entering the room. So lively was the antique boy that Agatha was rather alarmed at her own temerity when she considered what was the basis of his gaiety; wishing she could get from him some such writing

Assent – *Agreement*

Improbable – *Unlikely*

Temerity – *Boldness, Rashness*

Gaiety – *Merriment*

as he had got from her, that the words of her promise might not in any way be tampered with, or the conditions ignored.

"I only accept you conditionally, mind," she anxiously said. "That is distinctly understood."

"Yes, yes," said the yeoman. "I am not so young as I was, little dear, and beggars musn't be choosers. With my ra-ta-ta-say, dear, shall it be the first of November?"

"It will really never be."

"But if he doesn't come, it shall be the first of November?"

She slightly nodded her head.

"Clk! - I think she likes me!" said the old man aside to Aggy's uncle, which aside was distinctly heard by Aggy.

One of the younger children was in the room, drawing idly on a slate. Agatha at this moment took the slate from the child, and scribbled something on it.

"Now you must please me by just writing your name here," she said in a voice of playful indifference. "What is it?" said Lovill, looking over and reading. "'If Oswald Winwood comes to marry Agatha Pollin before November, I agree to give her up to him without objection.' Well, that is cool for a young lady under six feet, upon my word - hee - hee!" He passed the slate to the miller, who read the writing and passed it back again.

"Sign - just in courtesy," she coaxed.

"I don't see why--"

"I do it to test your faith in me; and now I find you have none. Don't you think I should have rubbed it out instantly? Ah, perhaps I can be obstinate too!"

He wrote his name then. "Now I have done it, and shown my faith," he said, and at once raised his fingers as if to rub it out again. But with hands that moved like lightning she snatched up the slate, flew up stairs, locked it in her box, and came down again.

"Souls of men - that's sharp practice," said the old gentleman.

"Oh, it is only a whim - a mere memorandum," said she. "You had my promise, but I had not yours." "Ise wants my slate," cried the child.

"I'll buy you a new one, dear," said Agatha, and soothed her.

Tamper – *Fiddle*
Coax – *Persuade*
Obstinate – *Stubborn*
Whim – *Fancy*

When she had left the room old Lovill spoke to her uncle somewhat uneasily of the event, which, childish as it had been, discomposed him for the moment.

"Oh, that's nothing," said Miller Pollin assuringly; "only play - only play. She's a mere child in nater, even now, and she did it only to tease ye. Why, she overheard your whisper that you thought she liked ye, and that was her playful way of punishing ye for your confidence. You'll have to put up with these worries, farmer. Considering the difference in your ages, she is sure to play pranks. You'll get to like 'em in time."

"Ay, ay, faith, so I shall! I was always a Turk for sprees! - eh, Pollin? hee-hee!" And the suitor was merry again.

VII

Her life was certainly much pleasanter now. The old man treated her well, and was almost silent on the subject nearest his heart. She was obliged to be very stealthy in receiving letters from Oswald, and on this account was bound to meet the postman, let the weather be what it would. These transactions were easily kept secret from people out of the house, but it was a most difficult task to hide her movements from her uncle. And one day brought utter failure.

"How's this - out already, Agatha?" he said, meeting her in the lane at dawn on a foggy morning. She was actually reading a letter just received, and there was no disguising the truth.

"I've been for a letter from Oswald."

"Well, but that won't do. Since he don't come for ye, ye must think no more about him."

"But he's coming in six weeks. He tells me all about it in this very letter."

"What - really to marry you?" said her uncle incredulously.

"Yes, certainly."

"But I hear that he's wonderfully well off."

"Of course he is; that's why he's coming. He'll agree in a moment to be your surety for the debt to Mr. Lovill."

"Has he said so?"

"Not yet; but he will."

Stealthy – *Furtive*
Bound – *Certain*
Incredulously – *Disbelievingly*
Debt – *Dues*

"I'll believe it when I see him and he tells me so. It is very odd, if he means so much, that he never wrote a line to me."

"We thought you would force me to have the other at once if he wrote to you," she murmured.

"Not I, if he comes rich. But it is rather a cock-and-bull story, and since he didn't make up his mind before now, I can't say I be much in his favor. Agatha, you had better not say a word to Mr. Lovill about these letters; it will make things deuced unpleasant if he hears of such goings on. You are to reckon yourself bound by your word. Oswald won't hold water, I'm afraid. But I'll be fair. If he do come, proves his income, marries ye willy-nilly, I'll let it be, and the old man and I must do as we can. But barring that - you keep your promise to the letter."

"That's what it will be, uncle. Oswald will come."

"Write you must not. Lovill will smell it out, and he'll be sharper than you will like. 'Tis not to be supposed that you are to send love letters to one man as if nothing was going to happen between ye and another man. The first of November is drawing nearer every day. And be sure and keep this a secret from Lovill for your own sake.

The more clearly that Agatha began to perceive the entire contrast of expectation as to issue between herself and the other party to the covenant, the more alarmed she became. She had not anticipated such a narrowing of courses as had occurred. A malign influence seemed to be at work without any visible human agency. The critical time drew nearer, and, though no ostensible preparation for the wedding was made, it was evident to all that Lovill was painting and papering his house for somebody's reception. He made a lawn where there had existed a nook of refuse; he bought furniture for a woman's room. The greatest horror was that he insisted upon her taking his arm one day, and there being no help for it she assented, though her distaste was unutterable. She felt the skinny arm through his sleeve, saw over the wry shoulders, looked upon the knobby feet, and shuddered. What if Oswald should not come; the time for her uncle's departure was really getting near. When she reached home she ran up to her bedroom.

On recovering from her dreads a little, Agatha looked from the window. The deaf lad John, who assisted in the mill,

Reckon – *Estimate*
Malign – *Damaging*
Unutterable – *Unspeakable*
Wry – *Ironic*
Dreads – *Fears*

was quietly glancing toward her, and a gleam of friendship passed over his kindly face as he caught sight of her form. This reminded her that she had, after all, some sort of friend close at hand. The lad knew pretty well how events stood in Agatha's life, and he was always ready to do on her part whatever lay in his power. Agatha felt stronger, and resolved to bear up.

VIII

Heavens! How anxious she was! It actually wanted only ten days to the first of November, and no new letter had come from Oswald.

Her uncle was married, and Frances was in the house, and the preliminary steps for emigration to Queensland had been taken. Agatha surreptitiously obtained newspapers, scanned the Indian shipping news till her eyes ached, but all to no purpose, for she knew nothing either of route or vessel by which Oswald would return. He had mentioned nothing more than the month of his coming, and she had no way of making that single scrap of information the vehicle for obtaining more.

"In ten days, Agatha," said the old farmer. "There is to be no show or fuss of any kind; the wedding will be quite private, in consideration of your feelings and wishes. We'll go to church as if we were taking a morning walk, and nobody will be there to disturb you. Tweedledee!" He held up his arm and crossed it with his walking stick, as if he were playing the fiddle, at the same time cutting a caper.

"He will come, and then I shan't be able to marry you, even th-th-though I may wish to ever so much," she faltered, shivering. "I have promised him, and I must have him, you know, and you have agreed to let me."

"Yes, yes," said Farmer Lovill, pleasantly. "But that's a misfortune you need not fear at all, my dear; he won't come at this late day and compel you to marry him in spite of your attachment to me. But, ah - it is only a joke to tease me, you little rogue! Your uncle says so."

"Agatha, come, cheer up, and think no more of that fellow," said her uncle when they chanced to be alone together. "'Tis ridiculous, you know. We always knew he wouldn't come."

Gleam – *Glow*
Preliminary – *Initial*
Surreptitiously – *Furtively*
Fuss – *Worry*
Falter – *Waver*

The day passed. The sixth morning came, the noon, the evening. The fifth day came and vanished. Still no sound of Oswald. His friends now lived in London, and there was not a soul in the parish, save herself, that he corresponded with, or one to whom she could apply in such a delicate matter as this.

It was the evening before her wedding day, and she was standing alone in the gloom of her bedchamber looking out on the plot in front of the mill. She saw a white figure moving below, and knew him to be the deaf miller lad, her friend. A sudden impulse animated Agatha. She had been making desperate attempts during the last two days to like the old man, and, since Oswald did not come, to marry him without further resistance, for the sheer good of the family of her uncle, to whom she was indeed indebted for much; but had only got so far in her efforts as not to positively hate him. Now rebelliousness came unsought. The lad knew her case, and upon this fact she acted. Gliding down stairs, she beckoned to him, and, as they stood together in the stream of light from the open mill door, she communicated her directions, partly by signs, partly by writing, for it was difficult to speak to him without being heard all over the premises.

He looked in her face with a glance of confederacy, and said that he understood it all. Upon this they parted.

The old man was at her house that evening, and when she withdrew wished her good bye "for the present" with a dozen smiles of meaning. Agatha had retired early, leaving him still there, and when she reached her room, instead of looking at the new dress she was supposed to be going to wear on the morrow, busied herself in making up a small bundle of ordinary articles of clothing. Then she extinguished her light, lay down upon the bed without undressing, and waited for a pre-concerted time.

In what seemed to her the dead of night, but which she concluded must be the time agreed upon - half-past five - there was a slight noise as of gravel being thrown against her window. Agatha jumped up, put on her bonnet and cloak, took up her bundle, and went downstairs without a light. At the bottom she slipped on her boots, and passed amid the chirping crickets to the door. It was unbarred. Her uncle, then, had risen, as she had half expected, and it necessitated a little more caution. The morning was dark as a cavern, not

Impulse – *Instinct*
Beckon – *Sign*
Confederacy –
Association
Caution –
Attentiveness

a star being visible; but knowing the bearings well, she went cautiously and in silence to the mill door. A faint light shone from inside, and the form of the mill cart appeared without, the horse ready harnessed to it. Agatha did not see John for the moment, but concluded that he was in the mill with her uncle, who had just at this minute started the wheel for the day. She at once slipped into the vehicle and under the tilt, pulling some empty sacks over, as it had been previously agreed that she should do, to avoid the risk of discovery. After a few minutes of suspense she heard John coming from under the wall, where he had apparently been standing and watching her safely in, and mounting in front, away he drove at a walking pace.

Her scheme had been based upon the following particulars of mill business: Thrice a week it was the custom for John and another young man to start early in the morning, each with a horse and covered cart, and go in different directions to customers a few miles off, the carts being laden overnight. All that she had asked John to do this morning was to take her with him to a railway station about ten miles distant, where she might safely wait for an up train. How will John act on returning - what will he say - how will he excuse himself she thought as they jogged along. "John!" she said, meaning to ask him about these things; but he did not hear, and she was too confused and weary after her wakeful night to be able to think consecutively on any subject. But the relief of finding that her uncle did not look into the cart caused a delicious lull in her, and while listlessly watching the dark grey sky through the triangular opening between the curtains at the fore part of the tilt, and John's elbow projecting from the folds of one of them, showing where he was sitting on the outside, she fell asleep.

She awoke after a short interval - everything was just the same - jog, jog, on they went; there was the dim slit between the curtains in front, and, after slightly wondering that John had not troubled himself to see that she was comfortable, she dozed again. Thus Agatha remained until she had a clear consciousness of the stopping of the cart. It aroused her, and looking at once through a small opening at the back, she perceived in the dim dawn that they were turning right about; in another moment the horse was proceeding on the way back again.

Suspense – *Mystery*
Custom – *Practice*
Weary – *Sleepy*
Lull – *Calm*
Interval – *Break*

"John, what are you doing" she exclaimed, jumping up, and pulling aside the curtain which parted them.

John did not turn.

"How fearfully deaf he is!" she thought, "and how odd he looks behind, and he hangs forward as if he were asleep. His hair is snow-white with flour; does he never clean it, then?" She crept across the sacks, and slapped him on the shoulder. John turned then.

"Hee-hee, my dear!" said the blithe old gentleman; and the moisture of his aged eye glistened in the dawning light, as he turned and looked into her horrified face. "It is all right; I am John, and I have given ye a nice morning's airing to refresh ye for the uncommon duties of today; and now we are going back for the ceremony - hee hee!"

He wore a miller's smock-frock on this interesting occasion, and had been enabled to play the part of John in the episode by taking the second cart and horse and anticipating by an hour the real John in calling her.

Agatha sank backward. How on earth had he discovered the scheme of escape so readily; he, an old and by no means suspicious man? But what mattered a solution! Hope was crushed, and her rebellion was at an end. Agatha was awakened from thought by another stopping of the horse, and they were again at the mill door.

She dimly recognized her uncle's voice speaking in anger to her when the old farmer handed her out of the vehicle, and heard the farmer reply, merrily, that girls would be girls and have their freaks, that it didn't matter, and that it was a pleasant jest on this auspicious morn. For himself, there was nothing he had enjoyed all his life so much as a practical joke which did no harm. Then she had a sensation of being told to go into the house, have some food, and dress for her marriage with Mr. Lovill, as she had promised to do on that day.

All this she did, and at eleven o'clock became the wife of the old man.

When Agatha was putting on her bonnet in the dusk that evening, for she would not illuminate her ghastly face by a candle, a rustling came against the door. Agatha turned. Her uncle's wife, Frances, was looking into the room, and Agatha could just discern upon her aunt's form the blue cloak which had ruled her destiny.

Blithe – *Casual*
Suspicious – *Distrustful*
Auspicious – *Favourable*
Discern – *Discriminate*

The sight was almost more than she could bear. If, as seemed likely, this effect was intended, the trick was certainly successful. Frances did not speak a word.

Then Agatha said in quiet irony, and with no evidence whatever of regret, sadness, or surprise at what the act revealed, "And so you told Mr. Lovill of my flight this morning, and set him on the track? It would be amusing to know how you found out my plan, for he never could have done it by himself, poor old darling."

"Oh, I was a witness of your arrangement with John last night - that was all, my dear," said her aunt pleasantly. "I mentioned it then to Mr. Lovill, and helped him to his joke of hindering you . . . You remember the van, Agatha, and how you made use of my name on that occasion, years ago, now?"

"Yes, and did you hear our talk that night? I always fancied otherwise."

"I heard it all. It was fun to you; what do you think it was to me - fun, too? - to lose the man I longed for, and to become the wife of a man I care not an atom about?"

"Ah, no. And how you struggled to get him away from me, dear aunt!"

"And have done it, too."

"Not you, exactly. The Parson and fate."

"Parson Davids kindly persuaded you, because I kindly persuaded him, and persuaded your uncle to send you to him. Mr. Davids is an old admirer of mine. Now do you see a wheel within a wheel, Agatha?"

Calmness was almost insupportable by Agatha now, but she managed to say, "Of course you have kept back letters from Oswald to me?"

"No, I have not done that," said Frances. "But I told Oswald, who landed at Southampton last night, and called here in great haste at seven this morning, that you had gone out for an early drive with the man you were to marry today, and that it might cause confusion if he remained. He looked very pale, and went away again at once to catch the next London train, saying something about having been prevented by a severe illness from sailing at the time he had promised and intended for the last twelve month."

Irony – *Satire*
Regret – *Remorse*
Hindering – *Delaying*
Admirer – *Devotee*
Pale – *Dull*

The bride, though nearly slain by the news, would not flinch in the presence of her adversary. Stilling her quivering flesh, she said smiling, "That information is deeply interesting, but does not concern me at all, for I am my husband's darling now, you know, and I wouldn't make the dear man jealous for the world." And she glided downstairs to the chaise.

Food For Thought

Miss Lovill, Agatha and Oswald, all the three were travelling in the same carriage. Oswald reciprocated Agatha's deep love for him and didn't mind her lie of hiding her real identity. Miss Lovill came to know everything about the poor Agatha and Oswald. What was her reaction? What happens at the end of the stroy? Why did Agatha marry Mr. David instead of Oswald Winwood?

Slain – *Killed*
Flinch – *To shrink*
under pain
Adversary
– *Opponent*

An Understanding

Q. 1. Who was Agatha Pollin and why was she addressed as Miss Lovill in the beginning of this story? Who was the young man who addressed her such and why did Agatha not disclose her real identity to him?
Ans. _____

_____

_____

_____

_____

Q. 2. From which place did the young man actually come from? What was he doing at Weymouth Esplanade? Who was Miss Lovill and how did this young man know her?
Ans. _____

_____

_____

_____

_____

Q. 3. Agatha felt guilty of not disclosing her real identity to the young and handsome, Oswald Winwood. Even Oswald was strangely attracted to her. Do you think they both were in love and what happened next?
Ans. _____

_____

_____

_____

_____

Q. 4. When did Agatha confess the truth that she was not Miss Lovill? Why did she feel it absolutely necessary to do so and what was the aftereffect?
Ans. _____

_____

_____

_____

_____

Joseph Conrad

Born on December 3, 1857

Died on August 3, 1924

Notable Works: *Almayer's Folly, An Outcast of the Islands, The Nigger of the 'Narcissus, Heart of Darkness, Lord Jim, The Inheritors,* etc. *The Black Mate, The Idiots, The Lagoon, An Outpost of Progress,* etc.

Early life

Joseph Conrad was born as Józef Teodor Konrad Korzeniowski on December 3, 1857 in Berdichev, Ukraine. He was a Polish novelist who wrote in English, after settling in England. Conrad is regarded as one of the great novelists in English, although he did not speak the language fluently until he was in his twenties (and then always with a marked Polish accent).

Joseph Conrad was born in Berdichev (Polish: Berdyczów), Kiev Governorate (now Berdychiv, Ukraine), into a highly patriotic, noble Polish family that bore the Nałęcz coat-of-arms. His father, Apollo Korzeniowski, was a writer of politically themed plays and a translator of Alfred de Vigny and Victor Hugo from French and of Charles Dickens and Shakespeare from English. He encouraged his son, Konrad to read widely in Polish and French. Conrad sailed up the Congo River in 1889.

Literary Works and Achievements

Conrad's adventurous life included dabbling in gunrunning and political conspiracy, which he later fictionalised in his novel, *The Arrow of Gold*. He apparently experienced a disastrous love affair that plunged him into despair.

Barely a month after reaching England, he signed on for the first of six voyages between July and September, 1878 from Lowestoft to Newcastle on a coaster misleadingly named *Skimmer of the Sea*. Crucially for his future career, he began to learn English from East Coast chaps. In 1883, he joined the Narcissus in Bombay for a voyage that inspired his 1897 novel, *The Nigger of the Narcissus*. In 1883, he joined the Narcissus in Bombay for a voyage that inspired his 1897 novel, *The Nigger of the Narcissus*. Some of his well-known works are: *Almayer's Folly, An Outcast of the Islands, The Nigger of the 'Narcissus, Heart of Darkness, Lord Jim, The Inheritors,* etc. *The Black Mate, The Idiots, The Lagoon, An Outpost of Progress,* etc.

Writing Style

Conrad, an emotional man subject to fits of depression, self-doubt, and pessimism. This disciplined his romantic temperament with an unsparing moral judgement. Writing in the heyday of the British Empire, Conrad drew upon his experiences in the French and later the British Merchant Navy to create short stories and novels that reflect aspects of a worldwide empire while also plumbing the depths of the human soul.

Later Years

For the remaining years of his life, Conrad was the subject of more discussion and praise than any other English writer of the time. He enjoyed increasing wealth and status. Conrad had a true genius for companionship, and his circle of friends included talented authors such as Stephen Crane and Henry James. In the early 1900s he composed a short series of novels in collaboration with Ford Madox Ford.

In April 1924 Conrad, who possessed a hereditary Polish status of nobility and coat-of-arms (Nałęcz), declined a (non-hereditary) British knighthood offered by Prime Minister Ramsay MacDonald.

Shortly after, on August 3, 1924, Conrad died of a heart attack. He was interred at Canterbury Cemetery, Canterbury, England, under his original Polish surname, Korzeniowski.

Trivia

In 1894, having served a total of 16 years in the merchant navy, Conrad retired from the sea to devote himself to a literary career. He had already begun writing his first novel, *Almayer's Folly*, while aboard the Torrens.

The Lagoon

~ Joseph Conrad

THe white man, leaning with both arms over the roof of the little house in the stern of the boat, said to the steersman,

'We will pass the night in Arsat's clearing. It is late.'

The Malay only grunted, and went on looking fixedly at the river. The white man rested his chin on his crossed arms and gazed at the wake of the boat. At the end of the straight avenue of forests cut by the intense glitter of the river, the sun appeared unclouded and dazzling, poised low over the water that shone smoothly like a band of metal. The forests, somber and dull, stood motionless and silent on each side of the broad stream. At the foot of big, towering trees, trunkless nipa palms rose from the mud of the bank, in bunches of leaves enormous and heavy, that hung unstirring over the brown swirl of eddies. In the stillness of the air every tree, every leaf, every bough, every tendril of creeper and every petal of minute blossoms seemed to have been bewitched into an immobility perfect and final. Nothing moved on the river but the eight paddles that rose flashing regularly, dipped together with a single splash; while the steersman swept right and left with a periodic and sudden flourish of his blade describing a glinting semicircle above his head. The churned-up water frothed alongside with a confused murmur. And the white man's canoe, advancing up stream in the short-lived disturbance of its own making, seemed to enter the portals of a land from which the very memory of motion had for ever departed.

The white man, turning his back upon the setting sun, looked along the empty and broad expanse of the seareach. For the last three miles of its course the wandering, hesitating river, as if enticed irresistibly by the freedom of an open horizon, flows straight into the sea, flows straight to the east - to the east that harbors both light and darkness. Astern of the boat the repeated call of some bird, a cry discordant and feeble, skipped along over the smooth water and lost itself, before it could reach the other shore, in the breathless silence of the world.

Grunt – *Sound*
Enormous – *Mammoth*
Immobility – *Motionlessness*
Expanse – *Area*
Entice – *Tempt*
Astern – *A backward direction*

The steersman dug his paddle into the stream, and held hard with stiffened arms, his body thrown forward. The water gurgled aloud; and suddenly the long straight reach seemed to pivot on its center, the forests swung in a semicircle, and the slanting beams of sunset touched the broadside of the canoe with a fiery glow, throwing the slender and distorted shadows of its crew upon the streaked glitter of the river. The white man turned to look ahead. The course of the boat had been altered at right angles to the stream, and the carved dragon head of its prow was pointing now at a gap in the fringing bushes of the bank. It glided through, brushing the overhanging twigs, and disappeared from the river like some slim and amphibious creature leaving the water for its lair in the forests.

The narrow creek was like a ditch: tortuous, fabulously deep; filled with gloom under the thin strip of pure and shining blue of the heaven. Immense trees soared up, invisible behind the festooned draperies of creepers. Here and there, near the glistening blackness of the water, a twisted root of some tall tree showed amongst the tracery of small ferns, black and dull, writhing and motionless, like an arrested snake. The short words of the paddlers reverberated loudly between the thick and somber walls of vegetation. Darkness oozed out from between the trees, through the tangled maze of the creepers, from behind the great fantastic and unstirring leaves; the darkness, mysterious and invincible; the darkness scented and poisonous of impenetrable forests.

The men poled in the shoaling water. The creek broadened, opening out into a wide sweep of a stagnant lagoon. The forests receded from the marshy bank, leaving a level strip of bright-green, reedy grass to frame the reflected blueness of the sky. A fleecy pink cloud drifted high above, trailing the delicate coloring of its image under the floating leaves and the silvery blossoms of the lotus. A little house, perched on high piles, appeared black in the distance. Near it, two tall nibong palms, that seemed to have come out of the forests in the background, leaned slightly over the ragged roof, with a suggestion of sad tenderness and care in the droop of their leafy and soaring heads.

The steersman, pointing with his paddle, said, 'Arsat is there. I see his canoe fast between the piles.' The polers ran along the sides of the boat glancing over their shoulders at

Ditch – *Trench*
Tortuous – *Twisting*
Impenetrable –
Impassable
Perch – *A resting place above the ground*
Glance – *Glimpse*

the end of the day's journey. They would have preferred to spend the night somewhere else than on this lagoon of weird aspect and ghostly reputation. Moreover, they disliked Arsat, first as a stranger, and also because he who repairs a ruined house, and dwells in it, proclaims that he is not afraid to live amongst the spirits that haunt the places abandoned by mankind. Such a man can disturb the course of fate by glances or words; while his familiar ghosts are not easy to propitiate by casual wayfarers upon whom they long to wreak the malice of their human master. White men care not for such things, being unbelievers and in league with the Father of Evil, who leads them unharmed through the invisible dangers of this world. To the warnings of the righteous they oppose an offensive pretence of disbelief. What is there to be done?

So they thought, throwing their weight on the end of their long poles. The big canoe glided on swiftly, noiselessly and smoothly, towards Arsat's clearing, till, in a great rattling of poles thrown down, and the loud murmurs of 'Allah be praised!' It came with a gentle knock against the crooked piles below the house.

The boatmen with uplifted faces shouted discordantly, 'Arsat! O Arsat!' Nobody came. The white man began to climb the rude ladder giving access to the bamboo platform before the house. The juragan of the boat said sulkily, 'We will cook in the sampan, and sleep on the water.'

'Pass my blankets and the basket,' said the white man curtly.

He knelt on the edge of the platform to receive the bundle. Then the boat shoved off, and the white man, standing up, confronted Arsat, who had come out through the low door of his hut. He was a man young, powerful, with a broad chest and muscular arms. He had nothing on but his sarong. His head was bare. His big, soft eyes stared eagerly at the white man, but his voice and demeanor were composed as he asked, without any words of greeting—

'Have you medicine, Tuan?'

'No,' said the visitor in a startled tone. 'No. Why? Is there sickness in the house?'

'Enter and see,' replied Arsat, in the same calm manner, and turning short round, passed again through the small doorway. The white man, dropping his bundles, followed.

Proclaims –
Announces
Propitiate – *Appease*
Discordantly –
Conflictingly
Eager – *Enthusiastic*
Demeanour
– Behaviour

In the dim light of the dwelling he made out on a couch of bamboos a woman stretched on her back under a broad sheet of red cotton cloth. She lay still, as if dead; but her big eyes, wide open, glittered in the gloom, staring upwards at the slender rafters, motionless and unseeing. She was in a high fever, and evidently unconscious. Her cheeks were sunk slightly, her lips were partly open, and on the young face there was the ominous and fixed expression - the absorbed, contemplating expression of the unconscious who are going to die. The two men stood looking down at her in silence.

'Has she been long ill?' asked the traveler.

'I have not slept for five nights,' answered the Malay, in a deliberate tone. 'At first she heard voices calling her from the water and struggled against me who held her. But since the sun of today rose she hears nothing - she hears not me. She sees nothing. She sees not me - me!'

He remained silent for a minute, then asked softly —

'Tuan, will she die?'

'I fear so,' said the white man sorrowfully. He had known Arsat years ago, in a far country in times of trouble and danger, when no friendship is to be despised. And since his Malay friend had come unexpectedly to dwell in the hut on the lagoon with a strange woman, he had slept many times there, in his journeys up or down the river. He liked the man who knew how to keep faith in council and how to fight without fear by the side of his white friend. He liked him - not so much perhaps as a man likes his favorite dog - but still he liked him well enough to help and ask no questions, to think sometimes vaguely and hazily in the midst of his own pursuits, about the lonely man and the long-haired woman with audacious face and triumphant eyes, who lived together hidden by the forests - alone and feared.

The white man came out of the hut in time to see the enormous conflagration of sunset put out by the swift and stealthy shadows that, rising like a black and impalpable vapor above the tree tops, spread over the heaven, extinguishing the crimson glow of floating clouds and the red brilliance of departing daylight. In a few moments all the stars came out above the intense blackness of the earth, and the great lagoon gleaming suddenly with reflected lights resembled an oval patch of night sky flung down into the

Dwelling – *Residing*
Ominous
– *Threatening*
Audacious – *Daring*
Conflagration – *Fire*
Abysmal – *Terrible*

hopeless and abysmal night of the wilderness. The white man had some supper out of the basket, then collecting a few sticks that lay about the platform, made up a small fire, not for warmth, but for the sake of the smoke, which would keep off the mosquitoes. He wrapped himself in his blankets and sat with his back against the reed wall of the house, smoking thoughtfully.

Arsat came through the doorway with noiseless steps and squatted down by the fire. The white man moved his outstretched legs a little.

'She breathes,' said Arsat in a low voice, anticipating the expected question. 'She breathes and burns as if with a great fire. She speaks not; she hears not - and burns!'

He paused for a moment, then asked in a quiet, incurious tone—

'Tuan . . . will she die?'

The white man moved his shoulders uneasily, and muttered in a hesitating manner—

'If such is her fate.'

'No, Tuan,' said Arsat calmly. 'If such is my fate. I hear, I see, I wait. I remember . . . Tuan, do you remember the old days? Do you remember my brother?'

'Yes,' said the white man. The Malay rose suddenly and went in. The other, sitting still outside, could hear the voice in the hut. Arsat said, 'Hear me! Speak!' His words were succeeded by a complete silence. 'O! Diamelen!' he cried suddenly. After that cry there was a deep sigh. Arsat came out and sank down again in his old place.

They sat in silence before the fire. There was no sound within the house, there was no sound near them; but far away on the lagoon they could hear the voices of the boatmen ringing fitful and distinct on the calm water. The fire in the bows of the sampan shone faintly in the distance with a hazy red glow. Then it died out. The voices ceased. The land and the water slept invisible, unstirring and mute. It was as though there had been nothing left in the world but the glitter of stars streaming, ceaseless and vain, through the black stillness of the night.

The white man gazed straight before him into the darkness with eyes wide open. The fear and fascination, the inspiration and the wonder of death - of death near, unavoidable,

Incurious –
Uninterested
Cease – *Finish, stop*
Mute – *Voiceless*
Fascination –
Attraction
Inspiration –
Motivation
Soothe – *Pacify*

and unseen, soothed the unrest of his race and stirred the most indistinct, the most intimate of his thoughts. The ever-ready suspicion of evil, the gnawing suspicion that lurks in our hearts, flowed out into the stillness round him - into the stillness profound and dumb, and made it appear untrustworthy and infamous, like the placid and impenetrable mask of an unjustifiable violence. In that fleeting and powerful disturbance of his being, the earth enfolded in the starlight peace and became a shadowy country of inhuman strife, a battlefield of phantoms terrible and charming, august or ignoble, struggling ardently for the possession of our helpless hearts. An unquiet and mysterious country of inextinguishable desires and fears.

A plaintive murmur rose in the night; a murmur saddening and startling, as if the great solitudes of surrounding woods had tried to whisper into his ear the wisdom of their immense and lofty indifference. Sounds hesitating and vague floated in the air round him, shaped themselves slowly into words; and at last flowed on gently in a murmuring stream of soft and monotonous sentences. He stirred like a man waking up and changed his position slightly. Arsat, motionless and shadowy, sitting with bowed head under the stars, was speaking in a low and dreamy tone.

'. . . for where can we lay down the heaviness of our trouble but in a friend's heart? A man must speak of war and of love. You, Tuan, know what war is, and you have seen me in time of danger seek death as other men seek life! A writing may be lost; a lie may be written; but what the eye has seen is truth and remains in the mind!'

'I remember,' said the white man quietly. Arsat went on with mournful composure.

'Therefore I shall speak to you of love. Speak in the night. Speak before both night and love are gone - and the eye of day looks upon my sorrow and my shame; upon my blackened face; upon my burnt-up heart.'

A sigh, short and faint, marked an almost imperceptible pause, and then his words flowed on, without a stir, without a gesture.

'After the time of trouble and war was over and you went away from my country in the pursuit of your desires, which we, men of the islands, cannot understand, I and my brother

Suspicion – *Doubt*
Lurk – *Prowl*
Placid – *Docile*
Strife – *Trouble*
Imperceptible –
Unnoticeable

became again, as we had been before, the sword-bearers of the Ruler. You know we were men of family, belonging to a ruling race, and more fit than any to carry on our right shoulder the emblem of power. And in the time of prosperity Si Dendring showed us favor, as we, in time of sorrow, had showed to him the faithfulness of our courage. It was a time of peace. A time of deer-hunts and cock-fights; of idle talks and foolish squabbles between men whose bellies are full and weapons are rusty. But the sower watched the young rice shoots grow up without fear, and the traders came and went, departed lean and returned fat into the river of peace. They brought news too. Brought lies and truth mixed together, so that no man knew when to rejoice and when to be sorry. We heard from them about you also. They had seen you here and had seen you there. And I was glad to hear, for I remembered the stirring times, and I always remembered you, Tuan, till the time came when my eyes could see nothing in the past, because they had looked upon the one who is dying there - in the house.'

He stopped to exclaim in an intense whisper, 'O Mara bahia! O Calamity!' then went on speaking a little louder.

'There's no worse enemy and no better friend than a brother, Tuan, for one brother knows another, and in perfect knowledge is strength for good or evil. I loved my brother. I went to him and told him that I could see nothing but one face, hear nothing but one voice. He told me, "Open your heart so that she can see what is in it - and wait. Patience is wisdom. Inchi Midah may die or our Ruler may throw off his fear of a woman!" . . . I waited! . . . You remember the lady with the veiled face, Tuan, and the fear of our Ruler before her cunning and temper. And if she wanted her servant, what could I do? But I fed the hunger of my heart on short glances and stealthy words. I loitered on the path to the bath houses in the day time, and when the sun had fallen behind the forest I crept along the jasmine hedges of the women's courtyard. Unseeing, we spoke to one another through the scent of flowers, through the veil of leaves, through the blades of long grass that stood still before our lips. So great was our prudence, so faint was the murmur of our great longing. The time passed swiftly . . . and there were whispers amongst women - and our enemies watched - my brother was gloomy, and I began to think of killing and of a fierce

Courage – *Bravery*
Idle – *Lazy*
Squabbles – *Quarrels*
Stealthy – *Furtive*
Prudence – *Far-sightedness*

death. . . . We are of a people who take what they want - like you whites. There is a time when a man should forget loyalty and respect. Might and authority are given to rulers, but to all men is given love and strength and courage. My brother said, "You shall take her from their midst. We are two who are like one." And I answered, "Let it be soon, for I find no warmth in sunlight that does not shine upon her." Our time came when the Ruler and all the great people went to the mouth of the river to fish by torchlight. There were hundreds of boats, and on the white sand, between the water and the forests, dwellings of leaves were built for the households of the Rajahs. The smoke of cooking fires was like a blue mist of the evening, and many voices rang in it joyfully. While they were making the boats ready to beat up the fish, my brother came to me and said, "Tonight!" I made ready my weapons, and when the time came our canoe took its place in the circle of boats carrying the torches. The lights blazed on the water, but behind the boats there was darkness. When the shouting began and the excitement made them like mad we dropped out. The water swallowed our fire, and we floated back to the shore that was dark with only here and there the glimmer of embers. We could hear the talk of slave girls amongst the sheds. Then we found a place deserted and silent. We waited there. She came. She came running along the shore, rapid and leaving no trace, like a leaf driven by the wind into the sea. My brother said gloomily, "Go and take her; carry her into our boat." I lifted her in my arms. She panted. Her heart was beating against my breast. I said, "I take you from those people. You came to the cry of my heart, but my arms take you into my boat against the will of the great!" "It is right," said my brother. "We are men who take what we want and can hold it against many. We should have taken her in day-light." I said, "Let us be off;" for since she was in my boat I began to think of our Ruler's many men. "Yes. Let us be off," said my brother. "We are cast out and this boat is our country now - and the sea is our refuge." He lingered with his foot on the shore, and I entreated him to hasten, for I remembered the strokes of her heart against my breast and thought that two men cannot withstand a hundred. We left, paddling downstream close to the bank; and as we passed by the creek where they were fishing, the great shouting had ceased, but the murmur of voices was loud like the humming of insects

Loyalty
– Faithfulness
Embers – *Ashes*
Refuge – *Protection*
Entreat – *Plead*
Hasten – *Rush*

flying at noonday. The boats floated, clustered together, in the red light of torches, under a black roof of smoke; and men talked of their sport. Men that boasted, and praised, and jeered - men that would have been our friends in the morning, but on that night were already our enemies. We paddled swiftly past. We had no more friends in the country of our birth. She sat in the middle of the canoe with covered face; silent as she is now; unseeing as she is now - and I had no regret at what I was leaving because I could hear her breathing close to me - as I can hear her now.'

He paused, listened with his ear turned to the doorway, then shook his head and went on. 'My brother wanted to shout the cry of challenge - one cry only - to let the people know we were freeborn robbers that trusted our arms and the great sea. And again I begged him in the name of our love to be silent. Could I not hear her breathing close to me? I knew the pursuit would come quick enough. My brother loved me. He dipped his paddle without a splash. He only said, "There is half a man in you now - the other half is in that woman. I can wait. When you are a whole man again, you will come back with me here to shout defiance. We are sons of the same mother." I made no answer. All my strength and all my spirit were in my hands that held the paddle - for I longed to be with her in a safe place beyond the reach of men's anger and of women's spite. My love was so great, that I thought it could guide me to a country where death was unknown, if I could only escape from Inchi Midah's spite and from our Ruler's sword. We paddled with fury, breathing through our teeth. The blades bit deep into the smooth water. We passed out of the river; we flew in clear channels amongst the shallows. We skirted the black coast; we skirted the sand beaches where the sea speaks in whispers to the land; and the gleam of white sand flashed back past our boat, so swiftly she ran upon the water. We spoke not. Only once I said, "Sleep, Diamelen, for soon you may want all your strength." I heard the sweetness of her voice, but I never turned my head. The sun rose and still we went on. Water fell from my face like rain from a cloud. We flew in the light and heat. I never looked back, but I knew that my brother's eyes, behind me, were looking steadily ahead, for the boat went as straight as a bushman's dart, when it leaves the end of the sumpitan. There was no better paddler, no better steersman

Clustered – Gathered

Jeer – To laugh at, Mock

Regret – Remorse

Defiance – Disobedience

Fury – Anger

than my brother. Many times, together, we had won races in that canoe. But we never had put out our strength as we did then - then, when for the last time we paddled together! There was no braver or stronger man in our country than my brother. I could not spare the strength to turn my head and look at him, but every moment I heard the hiss of his breath getting louder behind me. Still he did not speak. The sun was high. The heat clung to my back like a flame of fire. My ribs were ready to burst, but I could no longer get enough air into my chest. And then I felt I must cry out with my last breath, "Let us rest!" "Good!" he answered; and his voice was firm. He was strong. He was brave. He knew not fear and no fatigue . . . My brother!'

A rumor powerful and gentle, a rumor vast and faint; the rumor of trembling leaves, of stirring boughs, ran through the tangled depths of the forests, ran over the starry smoothness of the lagoon, and the water between the piles lapped the slimy timber once with a sudden splash. A breath of warm air touched the two men's faces and passed on with a mournful sound - a breath loud and short like an uneasy sigh of the dreaming earth.

Arsat went on in an even, low voice.

'We ran our canoe on the white beach of a little bay close to a long tongue of land that seemed to bar our road; a long wooded cape going far into the sea. My brother knew that place. Beyond the cape a river has its entrance. Through the jungle of that land there is a narrow path. We made a fire and cooked rice. Then we slept on the soft sand in the shade of our canoe, while she watched. No sooner had I closed my eyes than I heard her cry of alarm. We leaped up. The sun was halfway down the sky already, and coming in sight in the opening of the bay we saw a prau manned by many paddlers. We knew it at once; it was one of our Rajah's praus. They were watching the shore, and saw us. They beat the gong, and turned the head of the prau into the bay. I felt my heart become weak within my breast. Diamelen sat on the sand and covered her face. There was no escape by sea. My brother laughed. He had the gun you had given him, Tuan, before you went away, but there was only a handful of powder. He spoke to me quickly, "Run with her along the path. I shall keep them back, for they have no firearms, and

Firm – *Stable*
Fatigue – *Tiredness*
Mournful
– *Sorrowful*
Narrow – *Thin*

Greatest Love Stories

landing in the face of a man with a gun is certain death for some. Run with her. On the other side of that wood there is a fisherman's house - and a canoe. When I have fired all the shots I will follow. I am a great runner, and before they can come up we shall be gone. I will hold out as long as I can, for she is but a woman - that can neither run nor fight, but she has your heart in her weak hands." He dropped behind the canoe. The prau was coming. She and I ran, and as we rushed along the path I heard shots. My brother fired - once - twice - and the booming of the gong ceased. There was silence behind us. That neck of land is narrow. Before I heard my brother fire the third shot I saw the shelving shore, and I saw the water again, the mouth of a broad river. We crossed a grassy glade. We ran down to the water. I saw a low hut above the black mud, and a small canoe hauled up. I heard another shot behind me. I thought, "That is his last charge." We rushed down to the canoe; a man came running from the hut, but I leaped on him, and we rolled together in the mud. Then I got up, and he lay still at my feet. I don't know whether I had killed him or not. I and Diamelen pushed the canoe afloat. I heard yells behind me, and I saw my brother run across the glade. Many men were bounding after him. I took her in my arms and threw her into the boat, then leaped in myself. When I looked back I saw that my brother had fallen. He fell and was up again, but the men were closing round him. He shouted, "I am coming!" The men were close to him. I looked. Many men. Then I looked at her. Tuan, I pushed the canoe! I pushed it into deep water. She was kneeling forward looking at me, and I said, "Take your paddle," while I struck the water with mine. Tuan, I heard him cry. I heard him cry my name twice; and I heard voices shouting, "Kill! Strike!" I never turned back. I heard him calling my name again with a great shriek, as when life is going out together with the voice - and I never turned my head. My own name! . . . My brother! Three times he called - but I was not afraid of life. Was she not there in that canoe? And could I not with her find a country where death is forgotten - where death is unknown?'

The white man sat up. Arsat rose and stood, an indistinct and silent figure above the dying embers of the fire. Over the lagoon a mist drifting and low had crept, erasing slowly the

Haul – *Drag*
Afloat – *Floating*
Leaped – *Jumped*
Shriek – *Screech*
Indistinct – *Unclear*

glittering images of the stars. And now a great expanse of white vapor covered the land, flowed cold and gray in the darkness, eddied in noiseless whirls round the tree trunks and about the platform of the house, which seemed to float upon a restless and impalpable illusion of a sea; seemed the only thing surviving the destruction of the world by that undulating and voiceless phantom of a flood. Only far away the tops of the trees stood outlined on the twinkle of heaven, like a somber and forbidding shore - a coast deceptive, pitiless, and black.

Arsat's voice vibrated loudly in the profound peace.

'I had her there! I had her! To get her I would have faced all mankind. But I had her - and--'

His words went out ringing into the empty distances. He paused, and seemed to listen to them dying away very far - beyond help and beyond recall. Then he said quietly—

'Tuan, I loved my brother.'

A breath of wind made him shiver. High above his head, high above the silent sea of mist the drooping leaves of the palms rattled together with a mournful and expiring sound. The white man stretched his legs. His chin rested on his chest, and he murmured sadly without lifting his head—

'We all love our brothers.'

Arsat burst out with an intense whispering violence—

'What did I care who died? I wanted peace in my own heart.'

He seemed to hear a stir in the house - listened - then stepped in noiselessly. The white man stood up. A breeze was coming in fitful puffs. The stars shone paler as if they had retreated into the frozen depths of immense space. After a chill gust of wind there were a few seconds of perfect calm and absolute silence. Then from behind the black and wavy line of the forests a column of golden light shot up into the heavens and spread over the semicircle of the eastern horizon. The sun had risen. The mist lifted, broke into drifting patches, vanished into thin flying wreaths; and the unveiled lagoon lay, polished and black, in the heavy shadows at the foot of the wall of trees. A white eagle rose over it with a slanting and ponderous flight, reached the clear sunshine and appeared dazzlingly brilliant for a moment, then soaring higher, became a dark and motionless speck before it vanished into the

Impalpable
– Unclear
Undulating
– Rolling
Deceptive
– Misleading
Retreat
– Withdrawal
Dazzlingly –
Spectacularly

blue as if it had left the earth forever. The white man, standing gazing upwards before the doorway, heard in the hut a confused and broken murmur of distracted words ending with a loud groan. Suddenly Arsat stumbled out with outstretched hands, shivered, and stood still for some time with fixed eyes. Then he said,

'She burns no more.'

Before his face the sun showed its edge above the tree tops, rising steadily. The breeze freshened; a great brilliance burst upon the lagoon, sparkled on the rippling water. The forests came out of the clear shadows of the morning, became distinct, as if they had rushed nearer - to stop short in a great stir of leaves, of nodding boughs, of swaying branches. In the merciless sunshine the whisper of unconscious life grew louder, speaking in an incomprehensible voice round the dumb darkness of that human sorrow. Arsat's eyes wandered slowly, then stared at the rising sun.

'I can see nothing,' he said half aloud to himself.

'There is nothing,' said the white man, moving to the edge of the platform and waving his hand to his boat. A shout came faintly over the lagoon and the sampan began to glide towards the abode of the friend of ghosts.

'If you want to come with me, I will wait all the morning,' said the white man, looking away upon the water.

'No, Tuan,' said Arsat softly. 'I shall not eat or sleep in this house, but I must first see my road. Now I can see nothing - see nothing! There is no light and no peace in the world; but there is death - death for many. We were sons of the same mother - and I left him in the midst of enemies; but I am going back now.'

He drew a long breath and went on in a dreamy tone.

'In a little while I shall see clear enough to strike - to strike. But she has died, and . . . now . . . darkness.' He flung his arms wide open, let them fall along his body, then stood still with unmoved face and stony eyes, staring at the sun. The white man got down into his canoe. The polers ran smartly along the sides of the boat, looking over their shoulders at the beginning of a weary journey. High in the stern, his head muffled up in white rags, the juragan sat moody, letting his paddle trail in the water. The white man, leaning with both arms over the grass roof of the little cabin,

Merciless – *Cruel*
Abode – *Residence*
Midst – *Middle*
Weary – *Tired*
Stern – *Severe*

looked back at the shining ripple of the boat's wake. Before the sampan passed out of the lagoon into the creek, he lifted his eyes. Arsat had not moved. In the searching clearness of **crude** sunshine he was still standing before the house, he was still looking through the great light of a cloudless day into the hopeless darkness of the world.

Crude – *Rough, Raw*
Creek – *A small, narrow passage in the seashore*
Lagoon – *A body, of water cut off from the sea by coral reefs*

Food For Thought

The central theme of the story is that death is inescapable and that is why Arsat's love, Diamelen too dies at the end. The author feels that 'Love is just an illusion that makes us feel happy momentarily'. Do you agree with the theme? Answer in 'Yes' or 'No' and give appropriate reasons for your answer.

An Understanding

Q. 1. Who is the narrator of the story and what does he narrate to Tuan? In brief, what is the story all about?

Ans. _____

_____

_____

_____

_____

Q. 2. Arsat was in blind love with Diamelen and so he didn't wait for his brother, who fell into the enemy trap. Why do you think that he felt guilty throughout the story and realised that 'Love in nothing but an illusion?

Ans. _____

_____

_____

_____

_____

Q. 3. The author, Joseph Conrad stresses on lots of symbols and contrasts throughout the story like use of dark/light, black/white, sunrise/sunset, water/fire, movement/stillness, etc. Explain these symbols in context with the story.

Ans. _____

_____

_____

_____

_____

Q. 4. Why did Arsat feel that as long as Diamelen was alive, he was only half a man and after her death, Arsat became a complete man again?

Ans. _____

_____

_____

_____

_____

SELF-IMPROVEMENT/PERSONALITY DEVELOPMENT

All books available at www.vspublishers.com

HINDI LITERATURE

MUSIC (संगीत)

MAGIC & FACT (जादू एवं तथ्य)

ACADEMIC BOOKS

TALES & STORIES

All Books Fully Coloured

MYSTERIES (रहस्य)

All books available at www.vspublishers.com